Dreaming and Other Involuntary Mentation

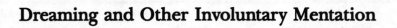

DREAMING AND OTHER INVOLUNTARY MENTATION
An Essay in Neuropsychiatry

By

Arthur W. Epstein, M.D.

International Universities Press, Inc.
Madison   Connecticut

Library of Congress Cataloging-in-Publication Data

Epstein, Arthur W.
   Dreaming and other involuntary mentation : an essay in
neuropsychiatry / by Arthur W. Epstein.
      p.   cm.
   Includes bibliographical references and index.
   ISBN 0-8236-1437-9 (hardcover)
   1. Neuropsychiatry.   2. Dreams.   3. Aphasia.   4. Neuropsychology.
I. Title.
   [DNLM: 1. Neuropsychology.   2. Neurons—physiology.   3. Dreams—
physiology.   4. Dreams—psychology.   WL 103.5 E64d 1996]
RC341.E68   1996
616.8—dc20
DNLM/DLC
for Library of Congress   96-23747
                                                                  CIP

Manufactured in the United States of America

Contents

11   Levels of the Unconscious   103

12   Dominant Networks: Imperative
     Fetishistic and Phobic Ideas   113

13   Dominant Networks: The Imperative
     Ideas of Obsessive–Compulsive Disorder   127

14   Origins and Transmission of Imperative Ideas   139

15   Implications for Psychodynamic Science   149

     References   159

     Author Index   167

     Subject Index   171

Preface

In an era witnessing the reuniting of psychiatry and neurology, we need correlations between elemental mental phenomena, dreams and ideas, and brain activity. Further, how can we express the nature of these phenomena in real terms, congruent with brain activity itself?

The two chief characteristics of neural tissue are connectivity and excitability. *Neural networks*, formed by the connective capacity of neurons, is a term now popular everywhere and, although herein called neuronal networks, is basic to this book.

Structures formed by the connectivity of associated items are endowed with varied degrees of excitability. Perhaps simplistically, the greater the excitability, the greater the likelihood the structure will act as a dominant neuronal network, the greater the likelihood mentation subserved by that network will be expressed in a powerful involuntary fashion, as an imperative idea.

These two concepts: associative structures (networks) and the excitability of these structures, are sufficient to make correlations with dreams and other involuntary mentation, and to do so in a fashion congruent with the physiology of the cerebral cortex. The two concepts permit understanding of mental phenomena, as is I hope demonstrated with the passage of this essay from the connectivity of aphasia, to the neuronal excessive excitability of epilepsy, to dreaming, to waking involuntary mentation, and finally to other considerations of psychodynamic science.

The data are clinical, obtained from my own experience and the literature. Many of the hypotheses gained seem well founded; others somewhat speculative. The purpose of this essay is to comprehend mental phenomenology, not to deal with specific treatments. However, since treatment must be based on the nature of the substratum treated, the reader will appreciate the rationale of many current therapies.

My activities in psychiatry and neurology have been stimulated, through the years, by Dr. Robert G. Heath, friend and mentor, founding Chairman of the Department of Psychiatry and Neurology at the Tulane University School of Medicine, a true pioneer in the correlation of mental and neural phenomena, and with the vision to create a department in which psychiatry, including psychoanalysis, and neurology exist under one roof

I am also indebted to Dr. Wayne Hill, now deceased, who worked with me on all-night sleep studies. Dr. Daniel K. Winstead, current Chairman of the Department of Psychiatry and Neurology at Tulane has furnished encouragement and support. Other formative teachers and colleagues are Dr. Joseph Globus, now deceased, Dr. Edwin A. Weinstein, Dr. Harold I. Lief, Dr. Russell R. Monroe, Dr. H. E. King, Dr. Frank Ervin, and Dr. Dabney Ewin. My thanks to Dr. Joseph Wortis, nurturing Founding Editor of *Biological Psychiatry*. I am indebted to Ms. Barbara Porter who typed and otherwise aided in the preparation of the manuscript. My wife, Leona, gave time latitude and support.

Figures 5.1 and 5.2 are reprinted by permission of the American Medical Association from Arthur W. Epstein and Wayne Hill (1966), "Ictal Phenomena During REM Sleep of a Temporal Lobe Epileptic." *Archives of Neurology*, 15:367–376. Copyright 1966 by the American Medical Association.

Figures 5.3 to 5.7 are reprinted by permission of Elsevier Science Inc. from Arthur W. Epstein (1979), "Effect of

Certain Cerebral Hemispheric Diseases on Dreaming." *Biological Psychiatry*, 14:77-93. Copyright 1979 by the Society of Biological Psychiatry.

For Figures 12.1 and 12.2, previously unpublished, I am indebted to Dr. Dan Knox, formerly Assistant Director of the Bernstein Park Zoo in Monroe, Louisiana, for his active participation and arrangement of photography.

Arthur W. Epstein, M.D.

1

The Fundamental Role
of Association (Connectivity)
in the Workings of the Mind

All organisms are bounded but require a means of dealing
with the space outside their boundaries. There must be a
means of approach, for example, toward nutriment, and of
avoidance away from harmful substances or predators. In
virtually all organisms, beyond the unicellular, this is accomplished by specialized cells—the neurons and their processes.

The simplest neuronal structure consists of a sensory
neuron transmitting external information to a motor neuron which then acts upon this information. In nature, there
are generally, even in the simplest systems, additional neurons interposed between the two, supplying some flexibility in response. As the evolutionary scale is ascended, there
is an increase in the number and differentiation of neuronal
aggregates.

In simple systems, sensorimotor activity is automatic
and stereotyped. Both observed behavior and its neuronal
substratum are reflexive in nature. It is possible, however,
to obtain some modification. Alkon (1975) repeatedly exposed the simple organism, Hermissenda, a mollusk, to

1

light, a stimulus mediated by photoreceptor cells, and followed this stimulus by rotating the mollusk, mediated by statocyst hair cells. After this procedure, cell recordings demonstrated hair cell responses to light flashes alone. What had occurred? A neuronal linkage had been established between cells mediating light and those mediating rotation. This linkage is established by the temporal contiguity of stimuli. The method exploits the natural tendency of neurons to link. The cells have "learned"; the "learning" results from alterations in the synapses between photoreceptor and hair cells. Such "learning" is called associative since an associative linkage has been formed between light and rotation.

This method of formation of associations (conditioning) was first demonstrated by Pavlov. A dog salivates at the sight of food. If a bell is repeatedly rung immediately before the food presentation, the animal will eventually salivate to the bell sound alone. The food is the unconditioned stimulus, the bell the conditioned. An associative linkage, a "temporary connection" in Pavlov's words, has been formed between the food presentation and the sound stimulus. Such a connection, believed Pavlov, is due to an actual anatomic path between different parts of the cerebral cortex. The path could be formed by changes in the neuronal dendrites, at the synapse or perhaps by other means.

Connectivity or the formation of associative linkages is a fundamental property of nervous systems. It occurs in primitive organisms without a well-differentiated nervous system but, despite anatomic and ideational elaboration, remains fundamental in all organisms. The human cerebral cortex, the most differentiated feature of mammalian cerebral structure, with its intricate cortical layering, its innumerable dendritic branchings, its synaptic plasticity, is well fitted to provide associative linking. The association of ideas, of memories, of images is basic in human mental life and is provided by the formation of cortical connections. Pavlov considered association at the mental level, "fully identical" with the conditioned reflex at the physiological level (Pavlov, 1957).

The first scientific step in the study of mentation was the recognition of associative mechanisms, first by Aristotle and later reaching further development in the British association school represented by Mill and Hartley among others (Mandler and Mandler, 1964). Associationists recognized that ideas were connected in an obligatory fashion by such factors as semantic or phonemic similarity, temporal contiguity, and successive order. Consider Mill's example of the binding of ideas in successive order.

After memorization of the Lord's Prayer, Mill states, "When we proceed to repeat the passage, the ideas of the words also rise in succession, the preceding always suggesting the succeeding, and no other. *Our* suggests *Father*, *Father* suggests *which*, *which* suggests *art*; and so on, to the end. How remarkably this is the case, anyone may convince himself by trying to repeat backwards, even a passage with which he is as familiar as The Lord's Prayer" (1878, p. 98). Such a binding suggests a tenacity of connection, neuronally determined (Epstein, 1994). The physician Hartley, more than two centuries ago, sought the neural substratum (the "vibrations") underlying associatively linked items. He thought "vibrations" had an anatomical locus and exerted energy.

Because humans have awareness of their mental content (consciousness) at a given time; awareness of voluntarily selecting certain content to exteriorize; awareness of voluntary decision making, there is a tendency to regard mentation as a purely voluntary activity. There is little appreciation of an obligatory connectivity constantly forming its web, a "cerebral reflex" action (Laycock, 1876). In short, this is mental activity not reporting to awareness (Rado, 1949), operating below awareness; this is the unconscious. There is little reluctance to accept the involuntary formation of connections at lower levels; for example, in the spinal cord but not in the brain. Being the possessor of the power of thought, there is an attendant hubris, assuming all thought is within one's possession, a disbelief that thought can be structured and bestowed, presented as a given by biological processes.

Freud's early neurological studies acquainted him with the importance of association formation in aphasia (Freud, 1891). He later divined the basic role of association formation, or connectivity, in human thought in general, particularly in dreaming. The method of free association was developed to unearth these associative threads. Freud's great contribution to association theory was his recognition of the influence of affects on the associative process. The painful feeling tone related to certain associative structures inhibits the activity of these structures in the sense of blocking their appearance in awareness (repression).

The nature of such a homeostatic mechanism able to inhibit the appearance in consciousness of certain associative structures requires a mental agency, later called by Freud the ego. This agency of regulation may operate voluntarily in awareness or in an automatic fashion below awareness (conscious and unconscious ego operations). Freud's hierarchy of the mind: conscious, preconscious, unconscious; later superego, ego, id is akin and was perhaps influenced by Hughlings Jackson's concept of nervous system levels. Neural levels of high complexity and late evolutionary development regulate, usually by inhibition, those of less complexity, and perhaps evolutionarily more ancient. Impairment of higher level inhibition releases the lower level. The released phenomena may prove unexpected and surprising. Who, for example, would predict such involuntary and uncanny movements as those of human chorea—movements released from higher controls? Jackson also applied his concept of levels to aphasic and epileptic phenomena (Jackson, 1958).

Hartley, Pavlov, Freud, and Jackson are seminal figures in the study of human mentation. Freud and Jackson were clinicians of the nervous system. In the pages to follow, aspects of involuntary human mentation will be viewed in the context of connectivity, from the clinical perspective. This view, perhaps one may call it the naturalist's view, will not employ statistical treatment of groups but will assemble observational data, interpret this data, and hope to arrive at meaningful syntheses, albeit at times somewhat speculative ones.

2

Associative Processes as Revealed by Nominal Aphasia

It is awe inspiring and somewhat bewildering for any anatomist when looking upon the immobile, finely sculpted human brain, to realize that this organ, made up of protoplasmic constituents, has the capacity to form language. Even when an anatomist goes beyond gross appearance and considers the microscopic neuronal aggregates and their energetics, mystery remains.

Somehow, in human evolution, the brain became able to shape sound waves into units conveying meaning; into words uttered, understood, and employed as tools of thought. How this transformation of sounds into words; of words into sentences obeying laws of syntax could have occurred is a source of wonder.

Brain tissue expanded as adaptive to survival needs of humanity. The specialized cortical and subcortical tissues necessary for language are placed, with few exceptions, in the posterior temporal-parietal and postero-inferior frontal regions of the left cerebral hemisphere. The language areas are supplied chiefly by branches of the left middle cerebral artery. Occlusions of this artery are likely to impair language function (aphasia).

Cases of nominal aphasia (naming impairment) illustrate processes of associative linking; for example, when

7

asked to name *chair*, the word *table* is uttered. Here, the precise name cannot be given. This paraphasic error is made because "chair" and "table" are associatively linked items within the semantic category of "furniture." Selectivity is impaired; the associatively linked item involuntarily intrudes. A second characteristic of nominal aphasia is the formation of neologisms (novel verbal units) usually from category related phonemic (sound units) and/or semantic fragments. A third is the involuntary repeated utterance (perseveration).

CASE FINDINGS

A 45-year-old, right-handed woman suddenly developed right hemiparesis and a nominal aphasia due to an occlusion in the left middle cerebral artery distribution. The event occurred in the year 1962. Imaging techniques were not then available to localize the left hemispheric lesion precisely. The hemiparesis quickly resolved, but the aphasia persisted and was studied through the years 1962 to 1964.

To test naming, objects were presented in serial order. Of the many objects presented, responses to only three are selected since they best illustrate principles of associative linkage. The three are: paper clip, safety pin, rubber band.

A paraphasic error, "pin," is made on presentation 24. Both paper clip and pin are inanimate objects and are similar in appearance and function. They are associated items within these three categories. The utterance "pin" is involuntary and obtrudes because of its associative linkage to "paper clip." The error is perseverated in presentation 27, the perseveration strengthened by the almost immediate prior presentation of safety pin. The error is also perseverated in presentation 29: further, the erroneous fragment, "pin" is combined with the fragment, "clip" to form the condensations "clin" and "clims." This condensed asso-

Presentation Order & Object	Response
62 Days Postocclusion:	
24. Paper Clip	Pin
	Clip
25. Safety Pin	Sen
	Tens
	Pin
27. Paper Clip	Pin
28. Safety Pin	Pin
29. Paper Clip	Pin
	Pin
	Pen
	Pick
	Pen
	Clin
	Clip
	Clims
39. Safety Pin	Clip
42. Paper Clip	Clim

ciative structure (a neologism) formed from the two fragments is perseverated as "clim" in presentation 42.

The error is perseverated in presentation 23. The precise name required cannot be voluntarily selected from the

Presentation Order & Object	Response
90 Days Postocclusion:	
23. Paper Clip	Pin
	Clip
24. Safety Pin	Safety Pin
25. Paper Clip	Clip

Presentation Order & Object	Response
111 Days Postocclusion:	
23. Paper Clip	Pin
	A Clip
24. Safety Pin	Safety Pin
25. Paper Clip	Clip
	Pin
	Pin
	Pin
	Clip
	Clip Pin
	Clip Pin
26. Safety Pin	Safety Pin
27. Paper Clip	Clip
	Pin

category. An associatively linked item intrudes and is uttered. The intrusion is overcome in presentation 25.

The paper clip is still misnamed as "pin" in presentation 23, displaying an adherence of linkage of "pin" to paper clip. In presentation 25, paper clip is named virtually correctly on first utterance but is then followed by the perseveration, "pin," again indicating inability to break the "pin"–paper clip linkage. Also in presentation 25, "clip" and "pin" are joined in utterance to form "clip pin."

As previously, safety pin is named correctly but never paper clip. First noted 111 days postocclusion, the words *pin* and *clip* (or its elaboration, *clipper*) are now linked. The inability to break the linkage results in such involuntary combinations (condensations) as "pin clipper" or "clipper with a pen." "Pen" is in a similar phonemic category as "pin."

Rubber band is also difficult to name. *Roll*, a word in related phonemic and semantic categories, intrudes and becomes joined, in presentation 42, to "pen," becoming

Presentation Order & Object	Response
146 Days Postocclusion:	
23. Paper Clip	Pin Clipper
24. Safety Pin	Safety Pin
25. Paper Clip	Clipper Pin
35. Safety Pin	Safety Pin
37. Paper Clip	Clip Pin Clip Pin Clipper Pin Clip Pin
40. Paper Clip	Clipper Pen Clipper with a Pen Clipper Pen Clipper Pen Pen
42. Rubber Band	A Rubber A Roll Roller Pen
44. Paper Clip	Clipper Pens Clip It with a Pen Pen Pen Rollers Roller with the Pens
45. Rubber Band	A Rubber Roller It's a Rubber It's a Rubber Rubber Roll
47. Rubber Band	Rubber with a Roll Rubber with a Band
48. Paper Clip	A Clipper A Clipper with a Roll It's a Clipper

Presentation Order & Object	Response
181 Days Postocclusion:	
1. Rubber Band	Rubber Roll
	A Roll
	A Roll Bell
	A Roll Beller
	A Rubber—But it's roll
	A Roll
	Rubber Bell
	Ripper
2. Paper Clip	Clipper Pen
	Pen
	Clipper Pen
	Clipper Pen

"roller pen." "Roll" or "roller" is perseverated in presentations 44 and 48 where they link to the paper clip errors as though there is a shared vulnerability of these items.

"Roll" remains as a perseverative paraphasic response. It then becomes linked to the paper clip neologism, forming a condensed neologism, "ripper." The involuntary adhesive linkage forming the neologism, "clipper pen" remains unbroken.

Presentation Order & Object	Response
209 Days Postocclusion:	
1. Paper Clip	Clip Pen
27. Paper Clip	Clipper Pen
35. Rubber Band	A Rubber
	A Rubber
	It's a Roll
	It's a Rubber

Presentation Order & Object	Response
251 Days Postocclusion:	
4. Paper Clip	Clipper
	Paper Clip
6. Paper Clip	Paper Clip
8. Paper Clip	Paper Clip
11. Paper Clip	Paper Clip
12. Rubber Band	Rubber
	Roll
	Roll Rubber
	It's a Roll Rubber
("It's a rubber band")	Rubber Band
14. Paper Clip	Clipper Pen
	Clipper Pen
	Clipper Pen
16. Rubber Band	Rubber Band
17. Paper Clip	Paper
	Paper
	Paper Clipper
	Paper Clipper
	Paper Clipper

The linkage forming the neologism, "clipper pen" persists. Rubber band continues to be misnamed with intrusion of the persistent fragment, "roll."

In presentation 4, the patient suddenly utters the correct name, *paper clip*. This is maintained for the next three presentations; then, returning to the adhesive associative linkage, "clipper pen." On the next presentation of "paper clip," the patient perseverates on the word *paper*, made in the earlier correct response, to produce, "paper clipper." The fragment, "paper," thus replaces "pen." After prompting by the examiner, the patient is able to cast aside the intrusive

Presentation Order & Object	Response
279 Days Postocclusion:	
1. Paper Clip	Clip Pen
	Clip Pen
	Paper Clip
2. Rubber Band	Rubber Roll
	Rubber Ball
	Rubber Ball
	A Rubber
	A Rubber Poll
	Rubber Ball
23. Paper Clip	Paper Climp
	A Paper Climp
	Paper Climp
	Paper Climp
25. Paper Clip	A Claper Pen
	A Paper Climp
	A Paper Climper
	A Paper Climmer
33. Rubber Band	Rubber Band
37. Paper Clip	Paper Climmer
	Paper Climmer
44. Paper Clip	Paper Clipper
	Paper Clipper
	Paper Clipper

fragment, "roll" and proceeds to name rubber band correctly on presentations 12 and 16. The neologisms "clipper pen" and "roll rubber" are thus altered perhaps presaging further improvement in the aphasia.

The very adhesive associative linkage, "clipper pen," ruptured twenty-eight days previously by entrance of the word, *paper*, remains ruptured. Indeed, in presentation l, the correct name, *paper clip* is given. Similarly, the correct name, *rubber*

Presentation Order & Object	Response
314 Days Postocclusion:	
1. Paper Clip	Clipper
	Paper Climmer
	A Paper Clipper
	Paper Clipper
	Paper Clipper
2. Rubber Band	Band Roll
	Rubber Band
25. Paper Clip	Paper Clipper
	Paper Clipper
	Paper Clip
27. Paper Clip	Paper Clip
35. Rubber Band	Rubber Band
39. Paper Clip	Paper Clip

band is uttered in presentation 33. This improvement in naming is coincident with loosening of the adhesive associative linkages; the patient is no longer bound to the involuntary linkages. Also noted is the use of the indefinite article, "a," introducing an apparent voluntary addition to the linkage.

Although there are traces of perseverative error, the positive trend, heralded 35 days earlier by the insertion of "paper" to rupture the adhesive associative linkage, continues. Indeed, both paper clip and rubber band are named correctly.

There are no traces of perseveration. Paper clip, rubber band, and all other objects are named correctly. Correct naming is maintained 377, 405, 433, and 503 days postocclusion.

On the 811th day, paper clip is named correctly, but unexpectedly, "rubber ball" is given as the name for rubber band. "Rubber ball" is in a related phonemic and semantic category to "rubber roll" and "rubber band."

Presentation Order & Object	Response
342 Days Postocclusion:	
1. Paper Clip	Paper Clip
2. Rubber Band	Rubber Band
26. Safety Pin	Safety Pin
27. Paper Clip	Paper Clip
35. Rubber Band	Rubber Band

Both paper clip and rubber band are named correctly 894 and 1062 days postocclusion. Since the naming impairment appeared resolved, examining sessions were then discontinued.

ASSOCIATIVE PRINCIPLES ILLUSTRATED

In this case, perseverative neologisms persisted almost a year after the development of the left hemispheric lesion. The neologisms represent associative linking of paraphasic fragments. The fragments are linked because they are members of the same semantic or phonemic categories. The involuntary persistence of the linkages may be attributed to two general conditions.

First, items associated by meaning or sound share a binding energy. This is a physical energy ("vibrations" in Hartley's sense). The second: a "higher" (in a hierarchical sense) center ordinarily regulating the binding energy is impaired. This dysregulation releases a more primitive level of organization—the emergence of crude, involuntary, tenacious associative binding. This "higher" energy, which in ordinary circumstances voluntarily selects and brings to utterance the correct name, is related to Head's (1926) "vigilance" function, defined as "high-grade physiological efficiency" in the cerebral sense or, in another parlance, high-grade activity of the "ego." The underlying neuronal energy binding items within categories, may be related to laboratory demonstrations of synaptic strengthening between neurons as produced, for example, by long-term potentiation (Bliss and Lomo, 1973). We also assume a physical energy underlying the "higher" activity regulating associative linking.

The role of category organization in aphasia is well documented. McKenna and Warrington (1978) described a patient, with left temporal lobe excision, whose ability to name "countries" was markedly superior to naming body parts, colors, animals, and objects—indicating relative preservation of the ability to name items within a specific semantic category. Warrington and McCarthy (1983) found, in a dysphasic patient due to left hemispheric infarction, selective preservation of food, animal, and flower items with selective impairment in the inanimate object category. Warrington and Shallice (1984) found visual identification and verbal comprehension of living things and foods impaired, inanimate objects selectively preserved, in four patients partially recovered from herpes simplex encephalitis. Hart, Jr., Berndt, and Caramazza (1985) reported an impairment in naming fruits and vegetables as compared to other object categories in an aphasic patient with left hemispheric infarction.

Basso, Capitani, and Laiacona (1988) found a category-specific naming and word comprehension defect (animals, fruits, and vegetables) in a patient with focal left hemispheric atrophic lesion. Such category-specific naming defects indicate that categories have specific anatomical substrata. Possessing specific substrata, categories may be selectively impaired by pathological processes (Epstein, 1992). Aphasia, then, particularly the nominal type, may be viewed as a disturbance in associative activity. This is in keeping with Freud's view (1891) that cerebral cortical speech regions are "an apparatus equipped for association."

Insight into the associative apparatus, derived from the nominal aphasic data, may be summarized as follows:

1. Associative mechanisms are involuntary. Formed beneath awareness, they are unconscious. Associative items are linked by a neuronal or interneuronal biochemical-physiological energy.
2. Associated items are organized into categories which, as "loops" or "networks," appear to have specific brain loci.
3. Associative structures are regulated by advanced brain areas whose influence is disconnected by the lesion.
4. The paraphasic error is due to the unbidden emergence of a category member.
5. Loss of regulation releases a lower level of organization characterized by a persistent and increased tenacity of binding between associated items, that is, by formation of perseverative neologisms.

3

Neuronal Excessive Discharge (Epilepsy): Categorical and Propagative Networks

The neurons of the brain seem always to be communicating, to be active, receiving and discharging, although the degree and location of activity vary with different states of the organism. In certain instances, a group of cells will discharge excessively. When excessive discharge becomes clinically manifest, it takes a form called epilepsy.

Epilepsy then is a manifestation of excessive neuronal discharge. This is regarded as a question of degree since the activity of cerebral cortical neurons is always subject to forces of both excitation and inhibition. Excessive neuronal discharge is potential in all nervous systems. A generalized convulsion, for example, can be induced in any human being by application of sufficient electrical energy as is the case with electroconvulsive therapy.

Excessive neuronal discharge and its propagation are the neurophysiological accompaniments of epilepsy. Discharge involving a central cerebral pacemaker, either moving centrifugally from the pacemaker to cortical and then spinal centers, or moving centripetally to the pacemaker from cortical cells and then centrifugally to cortical and spinal neurons, both produce a generalized seizure, a convulsion, a massive event. On the other hand, excessive discharge may be limited to specific cortical neurons or networks and not reach the subcortical pacemaker. This may be manifested as a partial seizure for which the patient is amnesic. The most common partial seizures are the complex partial. The temporolimbic area of the brain has a low threshold for excitability and is the area most involved in the production of complex partial seizures which may then be called temporolimbic seizures. The limbic area, phylogenetically older than the frontal and parietal neocortex, is the substratum for memory processing and for emotional experience and expression. Excessive discharges in this region therefore lend themselves to study of involuntary mentation and emotion.

Excessive temporolimbic discharge, escaping voluntary control, reveals features of associative processes; of the nature of associative networks; of images reflecting old events (memory); and of the influence of visceral and hedonic (pleasure-pain) feeling tone.

ASSOCIATIVE LINKING
AND CATEGORIZATION

The perseverative neologisms encountered in lesional aphasia may also be an epileptic event as, for example, described by Bell, Horner, Logue, and Radtke (1990), in a patient with a vascular malformation impinging on the left supramarginal and left posterosuperior temporal gyri (these are neocortical speech areas). Seizures began "with simple neologisms or strings of phonemes (phonemic jargon), which evolved readily into a copious flow of complex, reiterative, phonologically related neologisms" (p. 51). Examples of the ictal neologisms are: "severdedeen, exeverdedeen, exedrededeen." With seizures that occurred during monitoring, the electroencephalogram (EEG) showed rhythmic delta activity most prominent over the left posterotemporal region.

The seizures demonstrate phonemic stereotypy, almost always containing fusion and elaboration of the fragments, "ex" and "dedeen." The neologisms arise from fragments in the same phonemic categories. Here again, there is release of crude phonemic categories from higher control, in this instance due to epileptic excitation of the neural loci. Rather than a simple release, this might alternatively be characterized as an "overcoming" of regulatory higher centers. This epileptic case appears to confirm a neural locus for phonemic categories, one revealed by excessive neuronal discharge not, as previously, by the effect of a lesion.

Associatively linked items within semantic, more complex, categories may also appear due to excessive neuronal excitation. Hill and Mitchell (1953) described a patient in whom the words "a spade, a hoe or a fork," emerged during seizures. Here, the associatively joined items belong to the semantic category of implements. At an even more complex semantic level, an image appeared ictally always within the category of "someone wresting something from someone's grasp," for example, wresting "a stick from a dog; a rifle from the hands of a cadet; a hat from a hat check girl" (Kubie, 1953).

Associative items are bound to each other and share a biologic energy. This may be illustrated by a case of reflex epilepsy (Mitchell, Falconer, and Hill, 1954) in which temporolimbic seizures were evoked by looking at a "bright, shiny safety pin." A related object, scissors, had similar epileptogenicity. Pin and scissors are associatively connected within the same categories by virtue of semantic and, in view of their shiny surfaces, sensory similarities. Therefore, items A (safety pin) and B (scissors) are placed within a category, joined at the neural level, and endowed with a similar physiological power (Epstein, 1994).

In conditioned reflexology, the forming of a new association, a *temporary connection* in Pavlov's term, not only creates a new anatomic pathway (locus) in the cerebral cortex but also a physiological power. Pavlov spoke of such physiological forces as concentration of excitation or inhibition and irradiation of excitation or inhibition. A conditioning paradigm was used by Efron (1957) in an individual whose temporolimbic (uncinate) seizures were inhibited by the odor of jasmine. By repetitively staring, over an eight-day period, at a silver bracelet while smelling jasmine, an associative linkage was established. Eventually, staring at the bracelet alone and, finally, merely thinking intently about the bracelet, inhibited the seizures. Here, items A and B, associatively joined artificially, have equivalent physiological power. Item B (the bracelet) now linked to A (the odor) has by virtue of the forces binding associated items, become equivalent to A in physiological power, and thus is able, like A, to inhibit a focus of excess physiological power (an epileptic focus).

NETWORKS

As noted, categories have representation in specific cerebral cortical loci. Such a representation, containing associated items, may be called a circuit or a network. A network may be defined as an assemblage of neurons synaptically joined and subserving some shared function.

There is another type of network specific for epilepsy, namely the pathway of propagation of the epileptic discharge. Since the seizure manifestations in a given patient are usually the same and thus predictable, the excessive discharge should travel along the same neuronal network each time a seizure occurs. Propagative networks can be studied to advantage in temporolimbic epilepsy.

In his studies of epileptic propagation (the "march" of the excessive neuronal discharge), Hughlings Jackson (1958) described cases in which an olfactory or epigastric sensation was followed by involuntary ideation and imagery. In one case published in 1888, "the attacks began by smells, which he declared to be horrible." Further, "the patient had another preluding sensation—one seeming to start from the epigastric region." These visceral sensations were followed by an "intellectual aura" or "dreamy state": he "began to think of things years gone by, things intermixed—with what had occurred recently, things from boyhood's days." In addition, "peculiar sensations passing through his memory and appearing before his eyes. He thinks of things he has, might, or will do, he mentally sees people whom he has not seen for some years." Here, the involuntary mentation primarily consists of memories.

In a second case described in the 1888 publication, the propagation is first, vertigo; then, "strange smells and tastes" like chloride of lime; next his "dreamy state." He "seemed to actually see large buildings which he had once seen; it might be that he seemed near a church." He saw "certain alms-houses"; he "saw that building and could actually see the clock." When he did lose consciousness, it was "just after 'seeing' the buildings." Here, the images evoked are within a category, the category of buildings, again drawn from memory.

In a third similar case, published in 1890, autopsy revealed a neoplasm of the right temporal lobe involving the uncus and the extreme right temporal tip, which contains the amygdala. After this anatomic finding, discharges beginning with olfactory or epigastric sensations, then leading to the "dreamy state" become known as uncinate seizures. These were later subsumed under the broader classification of complex partial or temporolimbic seizures.

Later, Stevens (1957), in her study of forty patients with temporolimbic seizures, found epigastric sensations more common than olfactory, and also noted a frequent immediate following of the epigastric sensation by an inner experience of fear. Case 2 illustrates her method of content analysis with its progression: gastric—fear—bad odor; visions—threatening vision, death, fear—running, fighting, or smoking—generalized grand-mal seizure.

Kanemoto and Janz (1989) found that temporolimbic epileptic propagation follows definite patterns, although they are at times difficult to decipher. In their 143 patients, there is a high frequency of epigastric sensation. Epigastric sensation, anxiety, and visual hallucinations occur early in the unfolding sequence of propagation, while illusions of familiarity and aphasia occur late.

All studies on emotional experience in temporolimbic seizures find a high frequency of fear, little of pleasure. Dysphoria is common; euphoria virtually nil. In 100 patients who experienced ictal emotion, Williams's (1956) found 61 experienced fear, 21 depression, 18 either pleasant or unpleasant feeling tone. The preponderance of fear suggests that this emotion has great adaptive value in terms of individual and species survival. The occurrence of fear in seizure propagation indicates a locus for feeling tone within a network. Networks do not contain only ideational or imaginal loci but also affective components.

Outer expressions of affect, laughter, and to a certain extent crying, occur ictally but are usually bereft of an inner emotional accompaniment. In ictal laughter, no characteristic sequential pattern occurs, but there are motor accompaniments: massive movements of head, trunk, upper extremities; alterations in truncal posture or tone; facial vasomotor alterations. The truncal, and in some instances, outward and upward flinging upper extremity movements have been likened to those expressed, almost universally, in moments of triumph, possibly a release of a phylogenetic pattern (Epstein, 1985–1986). Stereotyped sequential patterns are also not evident in crying seizures, although rubbing of the head with the hand and head holding have been noted (Luciano, Devinsky, and Perrine, 1953), as has lateral head turning (Offen, Davidoff, Troost, and Richey, 1976). The former motor automatisms are consistent with those observed during grief in the waking state. Although offering promise for revealing the phylogenesis of these two ancient emotional states, the current data are not adequate for such network analysis.

Although propagation paths of epileptic discharge are often stereotyped and their manifestations predictable, the anticipated stereotypy may not always occur. The neuronal networks at play in epilepsy have some capacity for change. Such factors as the state of consciousness (sleep and waking), the nature of the origin of seizures, and their frequency may alter the firing route. In the course of epileptogenesis, certain network subsystems may be preferentially fired and thus become dominant. There may be expansion of networks through the recruitment of additional neurons (Faingold, 1992).

Again, certain forms of epilepsy are well recognized because they fire over specific networks, and indeed the recognition of such characteristic firing leads to clinical localization and diagnosis. Although this suggests species-specific similarities in paths of propagation, one must nevertheless consider a flexibility or plasticity of networks leading particularly to their expansion and to the development of preferential firing "strength" which may be called dominance.

Insight into the associative apparatus derived from the epileptic data may be summarized as follows:

1. Processes of associative linking and categorization described in nominal aphasia are confirmed by epileptic discharge phenomena.
2. A biologic energy is shared and exerted by associatively linked items within categories.
3. The presence and activity of neuronal networks are particularly evident in the propagation of epileptic discharge.
4. Characteristic networks of temporolimbic epilepsy display affective mechanisms and ideational–imaginal components of memory.
5. Although propagative networks are usually stereotyped, new concepts of network plasticity, including enlargement and dominance, are emerging.

4

Memory: Its Interplay with Neuronal Excessive Discharge

That neuronal networks through their excessive discharge may thrust memories into awareness, as in Jackson's description of the uncinate seizure (1888), is now a well-recognized feature of certain temporolimbic epilepsies.

A memory is the neural representation of an event occurring in the life span (ontogeny) and perhaps, but speculatively, in species history (phylogeny). The event must be registered and consolidated in the brain, placed into storage, and finally recalled.

Initial registration may be mediated by temporolimbic (hippocampal) systems; consolidation and storage by distributed cortical networks. No firm loci can be implicated for recall except for names which, as indicated in chapters 2 and 3, have a temporoparietal substratum. Registration, consolidation, and storage are involuntary as is recall, when the product of neuronal excessive excitation. However, recall may be voluntary. Volitional recall, a precise selective act, requires higher, likely frontal area, participation.

Memory is a survival necessity. Without memory, there is no avoidance of prior dangerous events; no approach to sources of food or other vital pleasure-giving situations. The integration of self, of "me-ness," the sense of identity, is built on the entire past store of memories. Memory's complete decay, then, results in loss of the inner experience of identity and the capacity to maneuver in the world outside.

Novelty is exciting; there is a specific hippocampal electrophysiological pattern for novel events. Familiarity creates less arousal. Also, there are events arousing by their very nature, those with unusual pain or pleasure. Memories of such events are vivid. Vivid memories, whether charged with pain or pleasure, produce a wish to reexperience, to be drawn to the internalized image of the event (the memory); a wish to reexperience the arousal. Finally, for ease of action, memories are stored in categories. As indicated previously, a specific category appears to have a specific neuronal locus.

EPILEPTOGENIC MEMORIES

A 14-year-old girl with generalized and complex partial seizures (since age 1) including lip-smacking automatisms, and with generalized spike and slow bursts on the EEG, was riding a merry-go-round at age 7 when she became dizzy. She saw her shadow and felt it might "get" her. The merry-go-round continued to circle; she looked at her shadow again and remained dizzy and weak. When arriving home, her grandmother fed her some corn. Two years later, suddenly and involuntarily, the entire scene appeared in consciousness. She "saw" the merry-go-round, the shadow, and the corn. This scene was immediately followed by a generalized seizure.

In this case, a memory of an affect-laden event involuntarily enters consciousness as the initial step in seizure propagation. The registration of this event is unique in that an altered physiological state was present, possibly a minor seizure, possibly neuronal activation by a moving visual stimulus. Registration of the event therefore occurred at the very time neuronal networks were in an altered physiological state. The memory was stored for a two-year period when the subserving network underwent excessive discharge resulting in its involuntary recall.

Why was this memory, or more properly its particular network, activated? Perhaps because registration occurred during an altered neuronal state destabilizing the registering network, making it more vulnerable to future excessive discharge. Perhaps because the event being registered had a strong affective quality, thus again producing a unique neuronal effect (Epstein, 1966).

A 14-year-old girl (Penfield and Rasmussen, 1950) experienced an intensely frightening event at age 7 when a man approached her and, in effect, threatened to put her in a bag containing snakes. Occasional frightening dreams followed in which the scene was reenacted. At age 11, the scene appeared involuntarily in waking consciousness followed, at times, by a convulsion. Operation revealed adhesions and atrophy in the right temporo-occipital region. In infancy, the patient had a convulsion.

Again, in this case, neuronal networks, subserving registration and storage of a highly affectively laden event, undergo excessive discharge thrusting the memory of the event into waking and dream awareness. Finally, the excessive discharge is sufficiently dominant and with sufficient recruiting strength to become the first component in a generalized convulsion. The network subserving the memory discharges to the extent that its propagation reaches a subcortical pacemaker. A predisposing neuronal instability (the infantile convulsion) is also present.

In three of Hill and Mitchell's cases (1953), a highly arousing, indeed a clearly traumatic event, was reproduced in subsequent seizures.

In example 1, a 20-year-old woman "described a vision of a nurse approaching her with a stomach tube" as a seizure component. Her seizures began at age 6 when, while hospitalized, she was tube fed.

In example 2, a 39-year-old man during seizures "raised his hand in front of his face, cowered, and said, 'Don't hit me, Dad, please don't hit me!'" In addition, as a seizure component, he reported "a visual scene of his father standing over him, threatening him with a poker." His seizures began at age 10 after he was struck with a poker by his father.

In example 3, a 49-year-old man saw in his seizures, "the cockpit of a burning plane in which two airmen were trapped." This scene was associated with "an epigastric sensation and a taste of burnt fish." Seizures began at age 40. At age 38 "he had actually witnessed this plane crash and was unable to help" (Hill and Mitchell, 1953, p. 720).

In these cases, a traumatic event preceded the onset of the seizure disorder suggesting that the event itself, perhaps due to the unique registration and consolidation of any sufficiently traumatic event, exerted an epileptogenic power. In these three, all with abnormal EEGs, there was no history of seizures before the traumatic event. It would seem the neuronal networks subserving the registration, consolidation, and subsequent storage of the event were, due to the arousing nature of the event, rendered excitable, remaining so through time, and as a function of that excitability, propagating and recruiting additional neurons until a clinically apparent seizure threshold was reached.

The long-standing presence of networks subserving emotionally laden memories and later becoming seizural was demonstrated by Penfield and colleagues (Penfield and Rasmussen, 1950; Penfield and Jasper, 1954). During neurosurgical procedures, electrical stimulation of the temporal lobe epileptic cortex elicited complex psychical reports representing memories that were also reflected in seizures and dreams.

The relationship of memory to neuronal excessive discharge was also illustrated by Lesse, Heath, Mickle, Monroe, and Miller (1955), from introspective data furnished by four individuals during subcortical and cortical recording. Electrodes were implanted by stereotaxis aided by ventriculography in accordance with Heath's (1954) method. Amplitude and frequency changes (well-demarcated moderate amplitude fast activity) occurred in amygdaloid and rostral hippocampal regions during reports of emotionally significant memories, most often unpleasant. These findings indicate that emotionally arousing, particularly painful, memories excite neuronal discharge in temporolimbic areas. Neuronal activation occurring with certain memories may then recruit and propagate until a frank seizure threshold is attained.

MEMORY IN POSTTRAUMATIC STRESS DISORDER

A relationship between memories of extraordinarily painful events and certain epilepsies leads next to consideration of the nature of such memories in the posttraumatic stress syndrome. In this syndrome, a biophysical uniqueness in the registration and subsequent processing of the overwhelmingly painful and survival-threatening event is assumed. The neuronal networks involved retain their excitability throughout time; their discharge underlies the involuntary appearance of the memory in the waking state and dream. Such unique processing of an overwhelming event insures lifelong vigilance. The memory is vivid, detailed, not modulated. The excitability of such neuronal networks, due to their "neurological strength," has been theoretically developed (Pitman, 1988).

That posttraumatic stress phenomenology reflects neuronal excessive discharge is supported by such examples as the case of an individual who served two years of combat in Vietnam and reported intrusive thoughts and nightmares (memories) of his war experience. Administration of carbamezepine, an antiepileptic and modulator of neuronal excessive discharge, ameliorated the nightmares (Stewart and Bartucci, 1986).

The repetitive involuntary appearance of a painful combat memory may, paradoxically, produce a wish to summon up, to reexperience the memory. Solursh (1988) interviewed twenty-two Vietnam veterans. In nineteen, involuntary combat memories were "highly exciting" and led to an apparent wish to reexperience the memory. Nadelson (1992) interviewed five Vietnam combatants with posttraumatic stress disorder. All expressed pleasure in the killing experience. One wished to reexperience his combat memories.

A memory is an internalization of an event. Any extraordinary traumatic event is accompanied by marked arousal and has been processed uniquely as a memory. Such a memory tends to produce, at higher levels, a wish for reexperience. The memory is endowed not only with painful feeling tone prompting avoidance but also with a pleasurable arousal component prompting approach. The excessive discharge intrinsic to neuronal networks subserving highly arousing memories results in network enlargement by recruitment, and, as a consequence, network dominance. Dominance may "attract" higher centers inducing voluntary reexploration. There is interplay between conscious volition and the involuntarily processed memory.

Insight into the interplay of neuronal excessive discharge and memory may be summarized as follows:

1. The imaginal memory of a catastrophic life event may become a component of an overt seizure. This may occur in an individual without preexisting overt seizures.
2. The memory of a catastrophic life event may appear involuntarily, awake, and in dreams not accompanied by overt seizures.
3. In both instances, the neuronal networks, subserving the memory, discharge excessively. The networks undergo a development from excitability to network enlargement (by recruitment) and dominance.
4. Activation of temporolimbic structures has been demonstrated physiologically accompanying the appearance of this type of memory trace.

5

Neuronal Excessive Discharge During Dreaming: The Recurrent Dream–Epilepsy Equivalence

The dream is the supreme example of involuntary mentation. Its elaborate sequencing, its presentation of long-forgotten memories, its surprises, its uncanny images have evoked wonder through human history.

How and why is a particular waking event selected for dream inclusion? How does new formation and disinhibition of associative linking produce dream content? Why are memories so accessible during the dream? How can there be such elaborate scenarios when the guiding thought is involuntary?

There are many wonderments and questions, but let us now continue the theme of previous chapters, that is, the effect of neuronal excessive discharge, as encountered in individuals with frank epilepsy, on the nature and content of dreams. As noted, a relationship between temporolimbic epilepsy and the dream mechanism was demonstrated by Jackson wherein excessive uncal discharge was associated with an unreeling of images, and by Penfield who found identity of seizure and dream content upon stimulation of epileptic cortex.

COMMON NETWORKS
IN SEIZURES AND DREAMS

1. A 38-year-old man (Epstein, 1964) had a recurrent dream since the age of 17:

> I am way up in the sky. There is a dark background, like night. There are all kinds of stars of different colors. They are multi-colored. There are moons, and I see the planet Saturn. I can tell that it is Saturn because it is turning and has a ring. I fall between these stars and moons. I fall and fall. All the time, my body is twisting this way and that. I never land. I feel as though I am trying to grab on to something but there is nothing to really grab on to. I never really strike earth. Then I wake up [p. 26].

This frightful dream occurred almost nightly but gradually decreased in frequency. At age 33, the dream began to occur while awake. At age 38, while awake, the dream suddenly appeared, immediately followed by dizziness, loss of consciousness, and a generalized convulsion. Waking EEG showed a paroxysmal left temporal abnormality.

In this case with left temporal localization, a discharging focus, a propagative network, appeared initially as a dream, only later revealing its epileptic identity by appearing as a waking prelude to a convulsion. A temporolimbic network discharging excessively recruits and propagates until it involves a central structure (secondary generalization).

The dream does not suggest a memory of a traumatic life event; it is accompanied by intense fear indicating limbic participation in the discharging network. The emphasis on colors and elementary visual forms suggests occipital participation; the falling and twisting, vestibular cortical participation. A recurrent dream therefore may or may not depend upon a previous waking traumatic event.

The relationship of recurrent dreams to temporolimbic seizures has also been noted by Clark (1915); Kardiner

(1932); Penfield and Rasmussen (1950); Rodin Mulder, Faucett, and Bickford (1955); Epstein and Ervin (1956); Epstein (1964); Ferguson, Rayport, Gardner, Kass, Weiner and Reiser (1969); and Reami, Silva, Albuquerque, and Campos (1991).

2. An 18-year-old woman (unpublished personal case) had a generalized seizure during sleep at age 11 immediately preceded by a dream: "My father was falling off a cliff. I tried to save him. I shouted 'Daddy, Daddy!' I tried to catch him. He disappeared."

This dream later appeared recurrently with further generalized convulsions. In the dream, a loved figure is endangered in a catastrophic fashion. Fear of loss of the supportive parent is expressed along with a likely ambivalent "wish" underside. The "falling" may represent excitatory phenomena in the dreamer's vestibular cortex (temporoparietal) projected to an external figure; the fear indicates a temporolimbic component. There is no indication that the dream represents a memory. The recurrent phenomena indicate stereotypy; the elements forming the neuronal network subserving this dream are adherent, closely bound.

3. A 34-year-old woman (unpublished personal case) had a recurrent dream from ages 5 to 11: "I'd be rocking in a rocking chair. The chair would be rocking faster and faster. A nail would be coming down the wire. Then it was like I was in a dirty cave. Then I was on some mushy stuff."

This dream was followed on at least one occasion by a generalized convulsion. The increasing tempo of the rocking imagery and the movement of the nail (a type of expectancy inevitable and uncontrollable) suggest cortical vestibular firing. The "dirty cave" and "mushy stuff" imagery may reflect higher level activity influenced by the incontinence which occurred during the seizure. There is no indication that the dream represents a memory of an actual event.

4. A 38-year-old man (Epstein and Freeman, 1981) experienced, while awake, the sensation of an episodic "warm

odor" beginning at age 15. At age 25, the "warm odor" was immediately followed by a generalized convulsion. Also, during the experiencing of the odor, which was accompanied by déjà vu, an observer noted the staring expression often encountered in a complex partial seizure. The "warm odor" also appeared in dreams (recurrent). When it does appear, "something disastrous" occurs in the dream imagery, for example, "If I am driving a car, I will have a wreck."

The olfactory sensation fits the uncinate seizure criteria described by Jackson. The dream imagery accompanying the olfactory sensation is unpleasant; the dreamer being endangered or injured. The appearance of an identical olfactory sensation in temporolimbic seizures and dreams indicates excitation of an identical neuronal network subserving dream and seizure. Although the déjà vu bespeaks involvement of the memory mechanism, there is no indication that the memories of actual events are represented in dreams or seizures.

CONTRIBUTION OF ALL-NIGHT SLEEP STUDIES

The discovery of the electroencephalogram (EEG), the discovery that dreaming occurs predominantly in the rapid eye movement (REM) sleep phase (Aserinsky and Kleitman, 1955), the discovery of characteristic EEG patterns delineating REM from other sleep stages (Dement and Kleitman, 1957), all coalesced to permit objective study of dreaming. All-night sleep studies have been applied to individuals with temporolimbic epilepsy and recurrent dreams.

5. A 35-year-old woman (Epstein and Hill, 1966) had generalized seizures from ages 12 to 13, then only complex partial (temporolimbic) seizures. The aurae consisted of "tightness in the stomach" and a "bitter taste." In an observed seizure, staring and searching eye movements with occasional swallowing movements were noted; after regaining full con-

sciousness, the patient reported that "tightness in the stomach" preceded the seizure. The patient has had painful recurrent dreams since childhood. Their content is elusive but in one, someone tells her she should be a nun. This dream was unpleasant and often accompanied by a "nervous cramping" epigastric sensation.

Two all-night sleep recordings revealed right temporal spiking. Repetitive spiking occurred during REM; indeed, rhythmic continuous spiking, preceded by a buildup of spike volleys, was recorded right temporally during all but one of eight REM periods. Even more remarkably, whenever the patient was awakened from a REM period during which the rhythmic right temporal spiking occurred, an unpleasant dream with epigastric sensation was reported; there were five such instances (Figures 5.1 and 5.2). Two are illustrated.

> Dream 1: I was with my brother. I wanted to wash the dishes and told my brother to feed the dog so I could wash the dishes. He wouldn't do it, so I jerked him. I had a nervous feeling in my stomach because I had done that to my brother. Then I dreamed that I saw my mother with a $20 dress. I felt sad because the dress looked too good for me. It was a $20 dress, but, in the dream, my mother had just paid $19 for it. My father was in the room, too, and I felt a nervous feeling in my stomach [p. 370].

The dream was unpleasant reflecting conflict with brother, and likely father; reflecting, as well, diminished self-esteem, and being "undeserving." "Jerking" the brother may reflect imagery derived from cortical motor excitation. An epigastric sensation accompanies the dysphoric content.

> Dream 2: I was at my aunt's house. I was sitting in a chair, and all the stuffing fell out. Mice ran under the chair and into the stuffing. One of my aunt's little girls said,

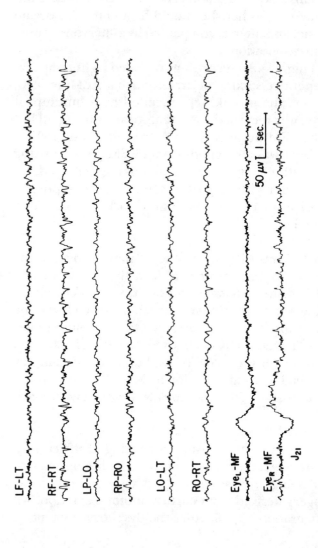

Figure 5.1 Rhythmic right temporal spike and slow activity during REM sleep prior to awakening from dream of brother. An REM is shown in the outer canthi leads at the beginning of this EEG fragment. F = Frontal, T = Temporal, P = Parietal, O = Occipital. L and R indicate left and right sides respectively. Eye L is the left outer canthus with the mid-forehead (MF) as reference; Eye R is the right outer canthus.

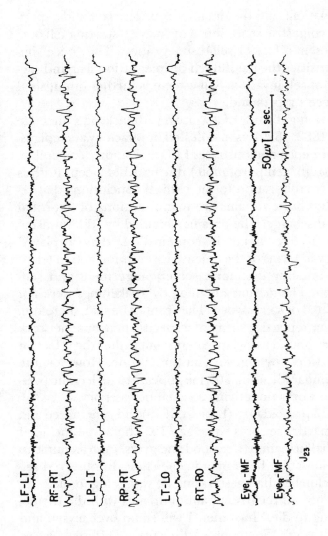

Figure 5.2 REM sleep with right temporal spiking and rhythmic slow activity 20 seconds before awakening from dream of mice. At least two REMs, appearing as slow deflections in phase reversal, are seen in the outer canthi leads. Note all leads contain a temporal derivation.

"You shouldn't drop all that stuff around to draw mice and insects" [p. 370].

The patient said the dream was unpleasant and experienced an epigastric sensation. The image, "stuffing fell out" may represent a fear of self-disintegration. The "mice" imagery intensifies the painful self-disintegration fear and suggests fear of self-invasion. Self-esteem is further diminished by the niece's reprimand.

This all-night study of a woman with Jackson's uncinate epilepsy (1888, 1890), as manifested by olfactory and epigastric components, demonstrates EEG activation of an epileptic focus (right temporolimbic) during REM sleep. It gives objective corroboration to the clinical conclusions that recurrent dysphoric dreams are manifestations of neuronal excessive discharge. The dreams obtained by REM awakenings were not recurrent in content. Yet, they displayed recurrency in terms of the epigastric sensation and in terms of theme, mainly dysphoric self-endangerment and self-diminution. The dreams obtained by awakenings were not impoverished or stereotyped. They cannot be said, therefore, to represent repetitive firing of a specific neuronal network with closely bound associative items; but rather the effect on varied networks by a given emotional tone. However, the dreams' similar ideational theme appears to reflect the presence of networks underlying a semantic category.

6. A 27-year-old man (Epstein, 1979) had generalized and complex partial seizures since age 10. The aurae included olfactory hallucinations ("seafood and grass") and an unpleasant body sensation beginning in the chest. In observed seizures, he clutched his chest, saying he was going to die.

He reported recurrent painful dreams with the theme, "I am going to die." In some, "I will stand over myself and see myself dying"; "Someone is killing me"; "Different people are getting killed." He had occasional dreams of disruption of the body image. "I saw my legs lying in one place and my shoulder lying in another place."

All-night recordings showed prominent right temporal theta–delta activity awake, during REM (where it appeared more rhythmic) and stage 1 sleep, disappearing in stages 2 and 3 sleep (Figure 5.3). Awakenings were made on nine nights from thirty-two of the thirty-seven REM periods identified. The right temporal abnormality appeared in all thirty-seven. A dream was reported in only three of the thirty-two periods.

Dream 1: Like I was dying—I told my mother I didn't have any pulse in my arm. She told me I wasn't dying. I was frightened. I could see myself dying. I was standing over myself.

Dream 2: I was going back to school. The home teacher took me out of school.

Dream 3: Like I was dying. Like I was telling my cousin that I was dying. Like I was dying; he was the one that died [p. 80].

During the study, an overt complex partial seizure occurred immediately following the night's final REM period; no dream was recalled (Figure 5.4).

These extended all-night studies of a man with temporo-limbic epilepsy (with uncinate components) is remarkable for the paucity of dream recall. All of the three dreams recalled are impoverished in imagery. Two are painful death dreams, identical in content and feeling tone to those described in seizures. The three dreams could not be differentiated on the basis of EEG features.

This study again reveals neuronal excessive discharge as manifested by EEG during REM sleep. The neuronal networks subserving the dying theme discharge both during overt seizures and recurrent dreams. The stereotyped and limited nature of the dying theme bespeaks a tightly bonded, yet dominant, network with restricted associative items in-

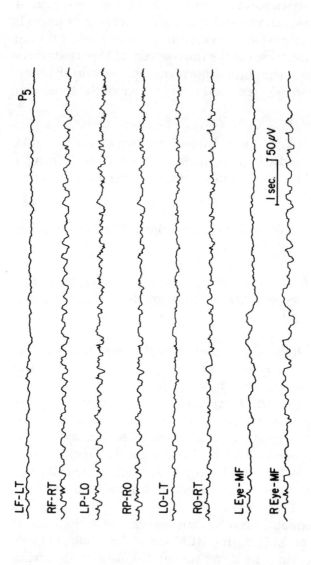

Figure 5.3 Rhythmic right temporal slowing (theta-delta), most evident over RF–RT derivations, during REM sleep. An REM (appearing as a slow deflection in phase reversal) is present in the outer canthi leads. Rhythmic slowing is also seen in the right outer canthus lead as a reflection of right temporal activity. When awakened from this REM period, there was no dream recall.

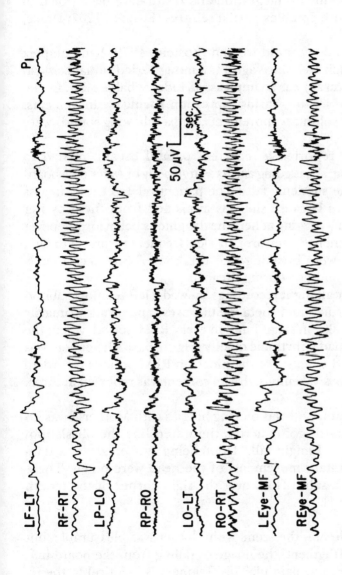

Figure 5.4 Right temporal paroxysmal activity accompanying complex partial (temporolimbic) seizure 135 seconds after termination of REM period. No dream was recalled.

fluenced by the strong emotion of fear. Ideation and imagery of bodily disintegration and death have been noted in others with complex partial seizures (Epstein, 1967; Drake, Jr., 1988).

7. A 35-year-old woman (Epstein, 1979) had complex partial seizures since age 11. Among varied initial seizural events (aurae) was an unpleasant, indescribable odor. In one observed seizure, staring expression, roving eye movements, clonic involuntary movements, and a "chewing sound" were noted.

She reported a recurrent painful dream, related to drowning; she is going across a large body of water on a board when she suddenly falls. The patient related these dreams to seizure because she was awakened from them by her daughter's tugging at her (the daughter's behavior whenever the patient had a seizure). In a less frequent recurrent dream, "people were breaking into the house." She occasionally smelled an odor during dreams.

Four all-night recordings showed a left temporal abnormality (spike and theta–delta waves) appearing primarily while awake, in stage 1 and in every REM period, where the slowing had a rhythmic quality (Figure 5.5). The patient was awakened from six of the nineteen REM periods recorded. Of the six awakenings, dream content was reported in three.

> Dream 1: "I was picking berries with Mother. I was on a board—going across the water, like the Mississippi River—I might fall." Upon being awakened, several involuntary movements of the head were noted. There was a saliva fleck over the right corner of the mouth [p. 84].

In this dream, the scene with Mother was pleasurable, but the last fragment, the image of falling from the board into the water, was painful. This fragment is identical to the recurrent dreams described in the history. As in the history, there are suggestive physical seizure signs accompanying this

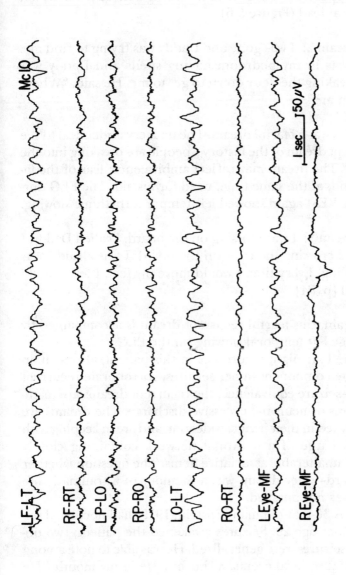

Figure 5.5 Rhythmic left temporal slowing (theta-delta) during REM period. A REM is present in the outer canthi leads. When awakened, the patient reported not dreaming.

dream. The seizural nature of this recurrent dream is further supported by the rhythmic slowing derived from the left temporal lead (Figure 5.6).

Dream 2: I was gone and Daddy was trying to find me. I was in my bedroom having spells and Daddy was breaking the door down to get to me. He said, "Where you at?"

This was a fearful dream. The imagery is identical to the recurrent dream of the history, "people are breaking into the house." The dream may reflect ambivalence; fear of the father, and, at the same time, need for his aid. The EEG during this REM again showed left temporal rhythmic slowing.

Dream 3: I was crossing on the board. I called Daddy. I was crossing the river on the board. I was afraid I was falling. Every time I would move my feet, I felt I would fall [p. 84].

Again, this fearful recurrent dream is accompanied by rhythmic left temporal slowing on the EEG.

The four night recordings in this patient, also with an uncinate component in her seizures, corroborate recurrent dream–seizure equivalence; the recurrent dreams are manifestations of neuronal excessive discharge. The dreams are stereotyped in their imagery-ideation and are in keeping with the discharge of a neuronal network containing closely bound, unalterable associative items. The question whether the board–water dream was a memory of a traumatic life event was not pursued.

8. A 30-year-old man (Epstein, 1979) had nocturnal seizures since age 29. Seizures awakened the patient; two observed seizures were generalized. He was able to note among the initial seizural events, a "burnt taste in my mouth." He reported recurrent painful dreams although these were not seizure components. "I have bad dreams, crazy dreams. I am

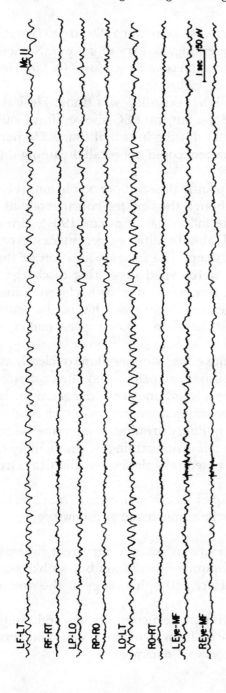

Figure 5.6 Rhythmic left temporal slowing (theta-delta) during REM period. REMs are not well shown although one is visible. When awakened, the patient displayed minor seizural phenomena and reported the "berry and board" dream.

in a cave, like closed up or something. You try to fight to get out. You are in something. You try to get out. Something closes up on you, sometimes under a house" (p. 90). He also had dreams of "being locked up."

Only one all-night recording was done. He was not awakened from REMs, but the EEG showed focal runs of rhythmic paroxysmal slowing in two of four REM periods (Figure 5.7). The patient could not recall dreaming during the night.

The recurrent painful dreams bore no obvious relationship to seizures although they existed concurrently as may be the case in some individuals (Epstein, 1964). However, the paroxysmal EEG abnormalities suggest sudden excessive discharge in REM sleep. The imagery-ideation of the recurrent dreams is stereotyped suggesting discharge of a dominant neuronal network, one with closely adherent associated items bearing the theme, that is, the semantic category, of immobilization in a closed space, endangering the dreamer.

Recurrent dreams either standing alone or clearly associated with a frank seizure have painful and often catastrophic content. The self or a loved one are endangered or dying. The imagery of the endangerment relates to such fundamental human fears as falling, drowning, being immobilized in a closed space, the self disintegrating, or an inability to resolve an arousing potentially dangerous physical circumstance.

The relationship of recurrent dreams to frank temporolimbic seizures may be summarized as follows:

1. As is true of dreams in general, recurrent dreams are examples of involuntary mentation but, unlike normative dreams, reflect pathophysiology of the dreaming process.
2. In certain individuals, recurrent dreams and temporolimbic seizures arise from an identical neuronal network in a state of excessive discharge.

Figure 5.7 Right hemispheric, chiefly right temporal, rhythmic slowing during REM period. REMs are not present in this fragment. The paroxysmal focal activity is terminated by muscle movement.

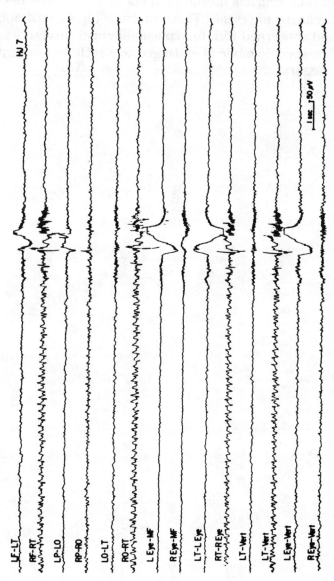

3. This neuronal network subserves stereotyped, closely bonded imaginal–ideational components accompanied by painful affect.
4. Painful recurrent dreams need not be actual memories of traumatic life events. Their content is often catastrophic and concerned with fundamental human survival fears. The specific mode of endangerment reflects a semantic category.

6

Neuronal Excessive Discharge During Dreaming: Connections Between Body Movement and Dream Imagery

Unlike recurrent dreams, associations in the normative dream are more fluid, darting to and fro. Fluidity indicates lifting of inhibition over associative activity. In dreaming, associative connections are newly created or, if not newly created, become available for new uses. Lifting of inhibition underlies the mechanisms of condensation (a confluence of connections often across categories) and displacement (a linking of one associative item to another closely related), mechanisms emphasized by Freud (1900) as fundamental in dream formation. Disinhibited associative activity is in keeping with the neuronal excitation known to occur in REM sleep (Hobson and McCarley, 1977).

This chapter will demonstrate how ease of associative connectivity links somatic sensations stemming from epileptic excitation with elaborate (symbolic) mentation.

1. A 20-year-old woman (Epstein, 1967) had nocturnal generalized (as described by her mother) seizures since age

13. Several weeks before seizure onset, an unpleasant dream appeared, became recurrent, and then an immediate seizure precursor.

DREAM (FIRST EVENT)

"My mother and father—they're both on different trains—coming the same way—toward me. They are both on the same track and coming to meet me. One is supposed to get there before the other. One of them is supposed to give me the ticket before the other. The wrong one is always getting there. I try to warn them."

"One night," the patient states, "I howled out (at the point where the 'wrong one' was getting there) and it was the spell" [p. 616].

With the passage of time, the recurrent dream ceased, replaced by a subjective sense of complex body movement again immediately preceding the convulsion.

ILLUSION OF COMPLEX
MOVEMENT (SECOND EVENT)

It feels as though my left leg is up in the air. I try to grab it. It seems like it is going up in the air. My leg has to go over my body and touch the floor. My whole body feels like it is turning over several times. It feels as though my left leg is trying to touch the floor and also as though something is trying to hold it back from touching the floor. I have to roll over several times before touching. My leg has got to touch the floor. Every time I touch my foot to the floor, I feel a sense of relief. It feels wonderful. It feels like I look forward to it when my foot will touch. At the moment that my left leg touches the floor, I cross my fingers and yell, "out." I feel alright when I do that. But then I pass out [1967, p. 617].

If considered alone, the manifest content of the dream (the first event) seems to represent the patient's competing love interest for her parents: to which parent to give priority. The parents are separated, and she wishes reunion. The ticket symbolizes resolution but the conflict is not satisfactorily resolved and the dream ends without fulfillment.

Both parents are endangered. The motion in the dream conveys a sense of urgency and expectation of inevitable disaster (an expectancy similar to case 3 in chapter 5). The mounting fear accompanying this expectancy cannot be resolved mentally and culminates in a seizure which "resolves" the impossible by loss of consciousness.

But if this dream is viewed in the context of the second mental event, as is proper since both are seizure events occupying the same position in regard to the oncoming convulsion, the somatic linkages of the dream can be detected. Indeed, the second event may also be considered a dream although it bears greater resemblance to a complex illusion of corporeal displacement.

The train is linked to the left leg.

The apartness of mother and father (they are on different trains) is linked to the sense of apartness of the left leg from the body (the left leg is "up in the air").

The movement on the tracks is linked to the movement of the left leg.

A wish to stop the onrushing trains is linked to the sensation: "as though something is trying to hold it back from touching the floor."

The need to get the ticket may be linked to, "My leg has got to touch the floor."

In the dream, a proper and safe arrival of the parents at their destination is not fulfilled contrary to, "Every time I touch my foot to the floor, I feel a sense of relief. It feels wonderful." The pleasure and fulfillment of the second event cannot be utilized by the dream synthesizer (the process of secondary elaboration) perhaps due to the severity of the conflict. The arrival of the trains at their destination is linked to the arrival of the left leg's touching the floor. Both the dream and the second event end with an emotionally laden vocalization.

The first event (a clear dream structure) precedes the second (a complex perceptual illusion). Therefore, the dream cannot be said to derive directly from the other, but both are mutually linked. There is an associative connection (a displacement) between body parts and their elaboration into the dream ideation. They are related recurrent phenomena.

The second event seems related to neuronal excessive discharge in the vestibular cortex. The dream of mother and father employs not only the vestibular cortex but also the higher participation necessary for construction and sequencing. This is the process of secondary elaboration or revision described by Freud (1900), perhaps one of the most advanced forms of involuntary mentation. Such high-order mentation would seem to require frontal lobe participation.

The vestibular influence on dreams is significant and has already been noted in cases 1, 2, and 3 of chapter 5. The intimate relationship between vestibular phenomena at the medullary–pontine level and their utilization at the frontal level has been emphasized by Hobson and McCarley (1977). The vestibular system is presumed to have a cortical locus in the superior temporal gyrus, bordering the parietal lobe. Epileptic illusions of body movement involving this locus have been reported (Ionasescu, 1960).

2. A 27-year-old man (Epstein, 1977) had a generalized seizure (observed) during sleep beginning with clonic movements of the right hand and with simultaneous dreaming. Dream: "My hand was coming off, and it started to bleed."

Shortly afterward, hypalgesia over the right upper extremity and right face were noted. The almost immediate juxtaposition of sensorimotor alterations in the right hand and a dream image about a hand indicates an associative linkage, undoubtedly long-standing, always established between a body part, particularly one as dominant as the right hand, and the image (idea) of the body part. An alteration in the hand and/or in the frontoparietal cortex subserving the hand, immediately evokes an image or idea of the hand.

Certain salient waking events of importance to dream formation are:

On one occasion, the patient cut his left hand.

Four years prior to the seizure, his 4-year-old son was killed in an automobile accident.

Increased sexual drive was noted a month prior to the seizure. He masturbated four or five times a day, even after having intercourse with his wife. He noticed "weakness of my right hand" during masturbation and used the left hand for this purpose.

The condensation of these varied elements to form the dream:

"My hand"

The altered sensorimotor state of the hand immediately activates the image or idea of the hand. Recent repeated masturbation has put affective focus on the hand. The hand may also be linked by symbolic meaning to the dead son (my son is my right hand) and may therefore represent the son.

"Was coming off"

This is linked to the clonic movements of the right hand, a product of epileptic discharge involving the left cortical motor strip. The image may also be linked by meaning to the recent repetitive masturbation since ejaculation is spoken of as a "coming off." The image also may be linked to the memory of the left-hand injury.

"And it started to bleed"

The clonic activity in the right hand and the memory of the cut left hand contribute to "blood" imagery as the mental representation of damage. The dream is occurring in a setting of catastrophic threat to organismal integrity, namely a seizure. The image of blood is accessed to represent such catastrophe. It might be said that blood imagery lies at a deep, ordinarily inhibited (repressed), level of unconscious mentation. Blood imagery has collective or archetypal qualities (Jung, 1953); all humans seem innately responsive to its sight.

In the two cases presented, body movements, primarily extremity movements, are linked via associative connections to the formation of a dream. The mechanism of condensation is particularly evident in the terse dream content of patient 2.

Any alteration in an extremity produces, by means of ascending sensory pathways, an effect on the cerebral cortex. Or, a threshold alteration in the motor cortex would be transmitted downward by corticospinal systems. The linkage, in any event, is bidirectional. In the dreaming brain where inhibition is lifted over associative activity, neuronal excessive discharge in motor or sensory cortex (posterior frontal or parietal) spreads to higher networks subserving imagery and its sequencing. Hobson and McCarley (1977) invoke such a process in dream formation, particularly signals produced by brain stem REM activation which provides higher cortical fields with input from oculomotor reticular and vestibular nuclei.

Ordinary small limb movements, as observed in the sleep laboratory, are related to limb actions reported in dreams (Gardner, Grossman, Roffwarg, and Weiner, 1975). The limb action may be the result of downward projection from the motor cortex but the opposite (upward projection to the brain from the limb) may also be operative. In either case, almost instantaneous associative pathways to higher centers forming the dream are employed. Somatic factors, peripheral or central, are therefore of importance in dream formation.

In dreaming, associative activity is disinhibited. The same may be true in psychopathologies as in the conversion disorder where there is sensorimotor associative connection to the semantic field. In conversion disorder, diminished "vigilance" permits such characteristic phenomena as "paralyzed" legs to be connected to mentation: "I cannot deal with this issue. I am so afraid. I cannot move my legs."

The theoretical significance of the case findings may be summarized as follows:

1. Through associative connections activated in REM sleep, there is mutual influence between body, particularly its extremities, movement, and dream mentation or imagery.
2. Such influence may be heightened in states of neuronal excessive discharge as in clinical epilepsy. Associative activity manifested as displacement and condensation, then woven by secondary elaboration, form the dream content.
3. Via associative activity, somatic factors form important components of dreams. The influence of vestibular activity is particularly noted.
4. Sensorimotor access to mentation due to associative disinhibition may be a factor in such psychopathologies as conversion disorder.

7

Typical Dreams: Dominant Networks Genetically Transmitted?

There are certain dreams common to all humans, cutting across cultural lines. These are called typical dreams, and as examples: something happening to the teeth; falling through space; the self or significant other hurt, in danger, or dead (the object endangered). Such dreams tend to be recurrent and opaque to interpretation by association (Freud, 1900; Ward, Beck, and Rascoe, 1961; Epstein, 1973b). An entire dream may be typical, or a typical theme may appear as a dream component. The widespread distribution of these dreams suggests three factors as causative: the sharing of common lifetime experiences (ontogenetic), the sharing of species experiences through genetic transmission (phylogenetic), the sharing of common somatic factors influencing imagery.

LOSS OF OR SOMETHING HAPPENING TO THE TEETH

1. A 26-year-old woman (Epstein, 1973b) experienced recurrent loss of teeth dreams of a frightening nature. These dreams are "real" like "my teeth are really coming out."

Dream 1: I was in the hospital. My teeth were coming out. It seems as though my tonsils were coming out. My teeth started coming out. As they were coming out, my tonsils started coming out and then my insides.

Dream 2: I was on a train or a bus. My husband was with me. There were beds on it. Every time the train would tilt, the beds would cross the floor. A piece of gum was stuck on my tooth. As I pulled the gum out, I pulled my tooth out. I thought, "It's really not a dream this time, it has actually come out." I wondered what it meant. I picked up a book. There were plastic figures on the book. A woman with a man on top. "This is me, I thought, this is why my teeth are falling out."

Dream 3: My mother was there with four men. They were looking at me, smirking. My mother gave me a sandwich. It was a hamburger. The hamburger had money in it. She wanted me to take the money to make me embarrassed. I ate the money sandwich and my teeth were coming out.

Dream 4: I was on a trip. I think I was alone. A motel room. My husband was there. He told me he was in love with someone else. I was trying to get him back. My teeth started to come out. I felt, "Gee, I am going to look ugly, all of my teeth are coming out." I thought, "Gee, I look ugly." Then my husband was not there.

Dream 5: Someone was trying to push me out of the house, trying to kill me. They had their foot in my back. Somewhere along there my teeth came out.

Dream 6: He went to the bathroom. A woman from downstairs came up and saw me in bed waiting. I was embarrassed because she knew I was waiting and wanting to be raped. With the confusion, the boys left and this woman came over and sat in the rocking chair next to my bed—I was showing her my loose teeth and accidentally pulled one out while doing that. Then they all started falling out and fell under the bed. I was on my hands and knees looking for them so I could save them in hopes they could be put back in. I asked this woman if this was really happening or was it a dream.

Dream 7: I felt I was going to vomit. I was vomiting. I was embarrassed and wiping it up. Then one tooth fell out. I said, "This is really not a dream—because I had this tooth." I put the tooth in my pocket because I was going to save it.

Dream 8: I had chewing gum stuck to my tooth. I knew I shouldn't pull it, but when I pulled it, it loosened the tooth and it fell out.

Dream 9: I was lying in the bed, trying to go to sleep. I kept hearing noises and was scared. My husband started kissing me. He was hurting me, he kissed me so hard. When he pulled away, he loosened my teeth. I went to the bathroom and looked into the mirror. My teeth were bent backward. I bent them the other way. Then I could close my mouth. Then I could taste blood and spit the blood out. I said to him, "Look at what you've done." My front teeth were all right, but I kept pulling out the back teeth. The back teeth kept getting bigger, as big as horseshoes [pp. 57–59].

In this individual, loss of teeth imagery occurs in varied dream settings; settings often painful involving sexuality and endangerment (the object endangered). Some dreams present purely mechanical (somatic) influences on teeth. The loss of teeth imagery is also associated with embarrassment, abandonment, and loss of physical attractiveness.

Whatever the setting or themes expressed, loss of teeth imagery intrudes in the dreams suggesting this imagery is subserved by a dominant network at low threshold for excitation. The elements of this network are closely bonded and stereotyped. The network may "discharge" at any time and then influence the processes of secondary elaboration (secondary revision) and associative connectivity. In dream 9, for example, the unfolding associations are: husband kissing me hard—he loosened my teeth—teeth bent backward—I bent them the other way—taste blood—spit blood out—look at what you've done.

Contrariwise, this low threshold network is available for expression of affectively laden memories or ideation. Significant ontogenetic experiences of this woman include: adoption with no knowledge of true parents, the sudden death of a foster father to whom she was attached, an unsatisfactory current marriage.

In this individual, somatic oral sensations are linked to loss of teeth imagery: gum adherent to tooth, eating, pressure of being kissed. In general, the sensitivity of the oral cavity and its contained teeth is exquisite. Here, one must consider the extensive representation of the trigeminal system in the brain and its capacity to access those higher centers which influence associative connectivity and sequencing.

2. A 22-year-old woman (unpublished personal case) experienced recurrent loss of teeth dreams of a frightening nature. These dreams are very real, "I feel it is actually happening." One fearful aspect is "teeth can never be replaced." She states, "I know in the dream that I will never have teeth again."

> Dream 10: "I would chew a piece of bubble gum. I go to take the gum out of my mouth. I couldn't get it out."

This was the first of the teeth dreams. The teeth are not actually falling out, but there is a sensation of their enmeshment in bubble gum.

> Dream 11: "I'd be going to talk. I can't open my mouth because, if I do, my teeth will fall out."

Dream 12: "I am talking. My teeth actually fall out and I catch them. It's not just thirty-two teeth that fall out but one-hundred eighty million of them."

Dream 13: "I run to my mother. I say, 'Mother, Mother, look, my teeth are falling out!' She says, 'Oh!' She is not excited."

Dream 14: "My left incisor tooth was falling out. I felt like it was on a string. It was only the one tooth that was falling out, but underneath it was another tooth. So if it fell out, it didn't matter."

Dream 15: "All my teeth are falling out."

In more recent dreams, the patient catches the teeth. This is encouraging because "When I catch the teeth, I am in hope of putting them back." There is also a reassuring aspect to dream 14 where a replacement tooth is available. Since the loss of teeth is catastrophic, such reassuring imagery is homeostatic (modulating) as is imagery of the flight to Mother's arms in dream 13. Oral somatic factors also serve as dream components: gum, opening mouth, talking. The recurrent loss of teeth dream in this individual again bespeaks a tightly bonded network of stereotyped items sufficiently dominant to make its entrance into dreaming.

3. A 24-year-old woman (unpublished personal case) experienced loss of teeth dreams.

Dream 16 (Abridged): Still I was looking for Room 217. Then I found it. The office reminded me of a bathroom the way it was set in with the other rooms. I knocked and called for Dr. X and he came out. When I was returning, he came with me and remarked about my being just out of high school. I told him with dignity that I was 26 (not true, I am 24). When we got off the elevator, we were in the lunchroom. There I saw my sister X's old schoolfriends who said I was always late for work in the past when I worked for V. R. Not true. Then the girl that works in the bookstore told me there was an election going on and that she voted for me, in fact, she stuffed the ballot box and I was sure to win. I was upset about this because it was dishonest. Then my tooth on the left side of my mouth just to the left of center started coming out. It felt like a baby tooth. I kept pushing it back in. A few other teeth were loose and I pushed them back in also—these were to the right.

In this dream, there is a long sequencing, much activity of the secondary elaboration, prior to loss of teeth imagery which occurs at the very end. This dream is cited to illustrate the sudden and unexpected appearance of the loss of teeth imagery, "pulled out of nowhere," a likely characteristic of a dominant circuit. The prior theme of the dream is the struggle against low self-esteem, the fear and expectation of criticism. In such a setting, the loss of teeth imagery may be confirmatory.

SOURCES AND POWER
OF CONDENSATION
OF TEETH IMAGERY

Loss of teeth dreams occur throughout humankind. The dream is interpreted according to the symbolic systems of the given culture. In Central Africa, the dream signifies "the dreamer will shortly lose his wife or child or other near relative" or "the dreamer's wife would bear a son who would grow up to be a strong man" (Hodgson, 1926). Loss of teeth imagery may serve as a focus for many connections, permitting condensation for expression of such ideation in contemporary Western society as: fear of loss of physical attractiveness, diminished self-esteem, fear of aggression, fear and/or wish for helplessness.

Although castration fears are prominent in psycho-dynamic conceptualizations, the literal imagery of genital loss is rarely encountered in dreaming in contrast to tooth loss. Teeth may be viewed as having greater individual survival value or are perhaps mentally encoded earlier in ontogeny. Later, loss of teeth may represent a castration displacement but this begs the question of the lack of genital imagery. The rich innovation of the oral cavity provides a potent somatic source for the dream. There is also one overwhelming fact which may account for the dream's ubiquity: all humans have experienced loss of teeth, the loss of the deciduous dentition. There is then an ontogenetic memory springing from a life event accompanied by youthful affect. Why this memory should be employed recurrently in later dream content, however, is not clear, although the potency of traumatic memories in creating neuronal excessive discharge has been discussed in chapter 4.

Again, one only rarely dreams of loss of penis or of arm and leg (an exception is case 2 of chapter 6, the dream here occurring in an epileptic setting permitting access to unusual levels of the unconscious). The more primitive meaning of teeth, perhaps with greater priority for encoding, is reflected in the mammalian heritage of humans. Teeth are essential for killing and eating prey and as a means of attack and defense. Later, in humans, teeth serve as objects of adornment and are of value in sexual selection.

A high level of tooth breakage has been found in large carnivores of the late pleistocene (Van Valkenburgh and Hertel, 1993). The modern elephant has three molar teeth that come into use one after the other; "when the last ones are worn out, the animal must of necessity die of starvation" (Aring, 1968). Aging male baboons lose their dominant social position, in part because of the wearing down of their teeth. In view of such vital functions, the breakage, loss, or wearing down of teeth must enter the awareness of high mammals and by some manner of genetic transmission, may be a factor in favoring the positioning

of teeth imagery into one of dominance in the human unconscious.

Loss of teeth dream imagery, then, serves as a focus of
strong condensation with associative connections contrib-
uted from somatic sources, ontogenetic memories, ontogenetic drives and defenses, and, speculatively, phylogenetic
roots. All of these connections are in keeping with the formation of a dominant network.

Because of the possibility that as a dominant network
with its features of recurrency, irregularities might be present
in the all-night EEG, a study was obtained in case 1 but did
not show epileptiform activity. This is in contrast to the cases
in chapter 5 in whom recurrent dreams, also typical, are
associated with clinical epilepsy and epileptiform EEGs.
Therefore, whether overt epilepsy or a seizural EEG are
present would seem to depend upon the degree of enlargement (recruitment) exerted by the dominant network.

FALLING THROUGH SPACE

An example of this typical dream is found in case 1 of chapter 5. To illustrate its universal presence, a dream of falling
through space, also with the typical theme of the self-
endangered, occurring in a man of the Yir Yoront, an Austra-
lian Aboriginal group (Schneider and Sharp, 1971) is cited.

> Dream 17: I was climbing up a blood wood tree to cut
> it for honey towards the top. I was knocking down dead
> limbs, cutting them from behind. Suddenly, I fell off,
> turning over and over and over (like a windmill—circle
> gestures with arm). I fell down, dead. Those bush people
> picked me up, a mythical ancestor (pa tangkain) picked
> me up in both arms. They all keened over me. They took
> me away, tied me up, and cut my knee tendons. I was
> suspended from the forked support and they eviscerated
> me. Then they put me in the ground and covered me

up. Then they all went back to camp in order to cry there. I was left behind and stood up. "Ah, I'm not dead!" My wife, Molly (Tum Lorn Pidlin), wanted to catch my hand, she was so glad. "He isn't dead any more! He's standing up!" [pp. 71–72].

Again, the sources of the "falling through space" dream may be viewed from somatic, phylogenetic, and ontogenetic aspects.

SOMATIC

The loss of stable body position, the sensation of falling and twisting, indicate loss of vestibular modulation (Jacksonian release), an excitation either in brain-stem vestibular centers or in the cerebral cortical representation of the vestibular system (Jackson, 1882). Since falling or extreme vertigo is always accompanied by fear, the limbic system would seem secondarily excited.

PHYLOGENETIC

To a large, striding, land-based organism with little capacity for climbing and none for flying, falling is a significant survival threat, particularly if the fall is extended, as in losing one's footing at a cliff edge. It would prove adaptive if humans were kept aware of this potentially fatal occurrence by dreams. In general, dreams accompanied by fear are adaptive in the phylogenetic sense as a means of alerting the individual to survival threats, preventing their actual occurrence in waking life.

ONTOGENETIC

Falling through space, as seems true of typical imagery, becomes a focus able to attract associative threads. The imagery may serve as a symbol for "falling" in the social sense as when status is threatened or as a symbol for sexual guilt. In

Central Africa, "to dream of falling through space signifies approaching sickness, but if the dreamer rises after the fall, he will duly recover" (Hodgson, 1926).

SELF OR ANOTHER HURT, ENDANGERED, OR DEAD

Examples of this typical dream are found in cases 2 and 6 of chapter 5. Another example is found in a mother's dream about her daughter (Epstein, 1987a):

Dream 18: Walking along. I think there's water. X (daughter) slips and starts to slip away. I can't catch her. She drowns. A very helpless kind of feeling [p. 409].

A remarkably similar dream, also involving death by drowning, was collected from a man of the Yir Yorunt (Schneider and Sharp, 1971).

Dream 19: My small son, Wol, drowned in the lagoon. He sank down in deep water. He fell from the bank into the water. Ducked in. Came up again. Ducked down again. Came up again. He kicked with his legs. He lost the strength in his legs. He went to this lagoon here from this camp. His eye came out. I cried, "My child!" I ran from the bank into the water and lifted up drowning Wol. I wept. I laid him down belly up. I called out, "My son!" Wol came to life again, he had really been a corpse. I pulled out grass to tie up Wol who was dead. I looked for my son to the southeast. I found him to the east. I said, "My child is to the east." Wol was over there defecating. I cried, "My child is alive; my real son." I put Wol on my shoulder and sang out to wife that son was alive. "Our son is alive." She said, "Good, our own son, husband." I said, "Really alive, wife" [p. 59].

SOMATIC

For the typical dream of endangerment or death, in general, no specific somatic focus can be implicated; the dream arises from ideational centers of the cerebral cortex.

PHYLOGENETIC

The prolonged human dependency period requires a protector; with increasing maturation, a wish to discard the protector—although the need always remains potential. The young one's survival depends upon parental, particularly maternal, protection. The dream of danger to the child alerts the mother to its actuality in waking life. Dependence on the parent, and in turn maternal protective behavior, are present through all vertebrates, evident to our eyes in avian, mammalian, and primate groups. Further, the social interdependence between humans is a phylogenetic given and would favor close bonding with resultant fear of loss.

ONTOGENETIC

Unique ontogenetic events may reinforce these phylogenetic factors and find expression in a typical dream: excessive dependence on a protective figure; premature loss of a protective figure; ambivalence with a wish to break the bond with a significant figure.

SOME OTHER TYPICAL DREAMS

TAKING AN EXAMINATION

The individual is about to take or is taking an examination. There is a feeling of unpreparedness, of not knowing or not finishing a question. The theme may be recurrent. There is no obvious somatic source of this dream.

Phylogenetically, an examination seems equivalent to an ordeal, to initiation rites so common in human societies. An ordeal is viewed ambivalently for there is a wish to succeed, to triumph but, at the same time, fear of failure and humiliation. Ontogenetically, most individuals have experienced such dreads and ambivalences. Being put to the ordeal is a source of profound anxiety but, at the same time, a test of the mettle of the self. The dream may serve as a focus, through associative connections, for other current conflicts.

MISSING A TRAIN OR PLANE

In this dream, there is a precise deadline to meet. Usually there is an obstacle, some disorganization preventing the accomplishment of the meeting. The theme may be recurrent. There are no obvious somatic sources. Phylogenetic factors are obscure. Deadlines have been important throughout human history. The dream may be related to anxiety over leaving or returning to a territory. Ontogenetically, most individuals have actually experienced the anxiety of not being able to be present on time for a necessary departure or arrival. The dream may serve as a focus, through associative connections, for other current conflicts.

BEING NAKED

The dreamer is naked or bereft of most clothing, yet onlookers show no apparent surprise, and there is little or no personal embarrassment. The theme may be recurrent, perhaps more common in younger age groups. The somatic sources of this dream are not clear. Phylogenetically, the dream may be related to humanity's long encounter with clothes and the impulses engendered; humans are the only clothed organisms. Ontogenetically, memories of donning and removing clothes are present in all lives. Deep erotic and exhibitionistic wishes find expression in nakedness. The dream imagery may also serve as a focus, through associative connections, for ideation related to social exposure, defenselessness, or infantile–childhood grandiosity.

BEING CHASED

The dreamer is in a state of fear as he or she is being pursued. There may be associated motifs of being harmed or robbed by the adversary. Limb movement may serve as a somatic source. Phylogenetically, being chased by human or animal must have been a frequent occurrence in species history. The experience of being chased, accompanied by fear and excitement, is also universal in ontogenetic experience. The dream may serve as a focus for varied ideation including ambivalent feelings toward sexual objects.

FLYING

The dreamer is flying or soaring in the air accompanied by pleasurable feeling tone but sometimes painful fear. The vestibular system would seem the primary somatic source. One can only speculate about phylogenetic possibilities. The human admiration and envy of birds in flight with a resultant avian identification is of ancient origin. Avian identification continues to exist in contemporary individual ontogeny. The flying imagery may be a focus for wishes of escape, liberation, and inflation of self-esteem.

RELATIONSHIP OF TYPICAL DREAMS TO OVERT EPILEPSY

Of the typical dreams cited, that of the object endangered has the closest relationship to overt epileptogenesis. This is illustrated in cases 2, 6, 7 and 8 of chapter 5. The dream of falling through space is also related to epileptogenesis (case 1 of chapter 5). There is no demonstrable relationship to overt epilepsy of dreams of loss of or something happening to the teeth; taking an examination; missing a train or plane;

being naked; being chased; flying. These findings suggest a catastrophic impact of the object endangered dream with a related capacity for enlargement, recruitment, and discharge of the underlying neuronal network.

The observations on typical dreams may be summarized as follows:

1. The universality and recurrent nature of typical dreams suggest they are products of dominant neuronal networks.
2. Dominant networks have a tendency toward recruitment and discharge. This is most evident in the dream of the object endangered which bears a clear relationship to overt epilepsy.
3. Typical dreams have phylogenetic roots related to their survival value. Typical dreams may also express significant affective phenomena in species history suggesting genetically transmitted "memory" networks.
4. Typical dreams serve as foci, condensation centers, for ontogenetic drives and conflicts as well as somatic sources.

8

Memory Processing and Category Building in Dreams

In chapter 4, it was shown that certain memories precede and then become components of overt epilepsy. These are memories of catastrophic events which, it is assumed, are encoded in the brain in a unique fashion endowing their subserving neuronal networks with overexcitability and, then, dominance due to the networks' capacity to enlarge. Enlargement and dominance imply that networks, or their neuronal elements, increase their connectivity and synaptic strength.

Dreams, in large part, grow from memories. Catastrophic memories may appear repetitively in dreams; this is a reflection of the dominance of their subserving neuronal networks. Can it be assumed that memories encoded not necessarily with catastrophic but nevertheless significant affect also make their way with ease into dream content? This cannot be proven for although a catastrophic event may clearly overcome modulating homeostatic forces, not any affectively laden event can do so. Such modulation, called "censorship" by Freud, is an inhibitory mechanism.

EARLY MEMORIES

A memory arising from an event, in childhood, would seem to have priority in the memory matrix since, at that time, neuronal

73

tissue is fresh, with less memories (except perhaps the phylo-genetic) already encoded. There is an opportunity for such chronologically young networks to gain strong connectivity and synaptic strength. Such networks might have an advantage in entering later dream structure. On the other hand, the contin-ued pressure of current memories requiring processing, would exert a dampening effect on the activity of the earlier.

Freud (1900) considered infantile memories a significant source of dreams. Adult dream content "may include impres-sions which date back to earliest childhood, and which seem not to be accessible to waking memory" (p. 189). The adult dream may not faithfully reproduce a whole and detailed childhood event; perhaps only a fragment may appear. This is similar to the loss over time of associative elements with preservation of only fragmentary items occurring in the ideational–perceptual phenomena (generally memories) comprising the temporolimbic seizure content described by Hill and Mitchell (1953).

Palombo (1984) systematically investigated the appear-ance of early memories in dreams, finding in forty-six of fifty consecutively reported dreams, a high incidence of early events. The earliest datable event occurred at age 2 years; the median age was 10 years.

In a larger sense, the total earlier experience rather than merely well-defined isolated events is reflected not only in dream content but in the warp-and-woof of the personality. It is not only the memory of childhood events but "we find the child and the child's impulses still living on in the dream" (Freud, 1900, p. 191).

A Dream Occurring in Adult Life

> A hill, on which there was something like an open-air closet: a very long seat with a large hole at the end of it. Its back edge was thickly covered with small heaps of faeces of all sizes and degrees of freshness. There were bushes behind the seat. I micturated on the seat; a long stream of urine

washed everything clean; the lumps of faeces came away
easily and fell into the opening. It was as though at the
end there was still some left [Freud, 1900, pp. 468–469].

Freud traces the various associative connections, the
latent thoughts related to the manifest dream content including a pleasurable identification with Hercules, as cleanser
of the Augean stables and with Gargantua wreaking revenge
by turning his stream on the Parisian streets below. The
dream can be clearly analyzed but, we ask, why these particular manifest images? Why these images from which, during the waking state, we would avert our eyes and thoughts?
The answer lies in the impulses and fascinations of early
childhood, when there is open and uninhibited interest in
the lower body and its products. This interest is partly determined by phylogenetic factors which direct attention to this
future zone for species survival. Interest in the reproductive
zones is never lost but draws inhibition in later life. The early
encoding of the oral, anal, and phallic areas, and their uses,
ensures their solid grounding in the mind or, in another parlance, ensures the dominance of their subserving neuronal
networks. These networks sustain inhibition but are able to
appear in the adult's dream, their crude nature often puz-
zling to the dreamer on awakening, because of lifting of inhibition (repression) in the dream state. Their appearance
requires a considerable weakening of inhibition since these
early states with strong priority for expression might prove
overwhelming without strong inhibitory forces arrayed
against them. Here, one enters the area of taboo with its ambivalences, its strong prohibitions and drives (Freud, 1913).

EARLY AND CURRENT
MEMORIES

Common observation attests to the appearance of early
memories in dreams—dream images of long dead parents and

other bygone, deeply bonded individuals are frequent. But, there is also a daily bombardment of current stimuli, memories newly forming. How are the two reconciled? Palombo's work (1978) describing a matching process, generated by the dream, between early and current memories, provides a solution.

Indeed, in waking life itself, there is a push to match, to compare a new event, almost immediately after its occurrence, with the memory of a similar older event; an associative connecting process strengthening the cohesion of categorization. This waking process is voluntary, a voluntary search through the memory store for a suitable linked item. A similar, but involuntary mechanism, occurs in the dream (Palombo, 1978).

Palombo notes the necessity of matching the incoming flow of daily events with earlier memories already embedded in the permanent store. This necessity is accomplished by the dream. Only some items of the incoming flow are included in the night's dream content; these items are known as the day residue. Since these day residue items can be identified in the dream content, an associative connection must have been made between them and items from the earlier embedded memory store; items related by semantic or other association, a shared categorization.

DÉJÀ VU

An automatic involuntary matching mechanism seeking to connect an immediate event with an older memory in the same category, may throw light on the nature of déjà vu ("already seen"), which is experienced as a sense of familiarity: "this has happened before" or "I've been here before."

Déjà vu is a relatively frequent symptom of epileptic discharge in the temporolimbic region; an area related to memory processing. Since déjà vu occurs in a setting of neuronal excessive discharge, its appearance must reflect a neuronal dysregulation. In déjà vu a new, an immediately current perception, is being compared to an earlier memory. The dysregulation unmasks the very process normally occurring in waking event/dream image processing; the matching of a current waking event with an older memory; the process making a waking event the day residue of a dream. The temporolimbic discharge, producing déjà vu, may allow access to the dream mechanism itself. Indeed, dream and temporolimbic seizure discharge seem to have the same locus, as noted in chapter 5. Therefore, the déjà vu sense of familiarity occurs because the immediate perception is, with great speed, finding and being connected to an older memory item, an item related and in the same category.

THE DAY RESIDUE

There is a neural rhythm to the dream process. Not only do REM periods occur on a regular cyclic basis but incorporation of the waking event into the dream (the day residue) also follows a cyclic rhythm. The waking event to be incorporated generally occurs on the day of the dream although, not infrequently, two to four days earlier (Epstein, 1985).

How a particular event of the innumerable events that occur daily is chosen for dream incorporation remains a mystery. An event or thought may appear neutral or indifferent and yet is selected. An indifferent event, Freud (1900) thought, might more readily serve as a vehicle for the discharge of older affectively significant material. Palombo (1978) thought events are selected which provide information of importance to the permanent memory store. On the other hand, it is possible that events are randomly selected providing a mechanism for widespread sampling of the waking environment; random scanning would incorporate information in a flexible manner.

Waking Event	Dream Image
Blond woman	A different blond woman
Indian neurologist	Indian psychoanalyst
Man with amputation below knee	Woman with bifid leg below knee
My two sons are at the table	Two other, younger boys are wrestling

It runs against intuitive expectations that an affectively laden waking event does not become an overt component of the day residue. This may represent, besides a random environmental scanning mechanism, an instance of homeostatic modulation (a term preferable to censorship). The dream mechanism may be more concerned with its routine sampling and memory processing tasks.

Tracing back from dream image to day residue, one finds the waking event is reproduced directly in the dream or, in many instances, may be slightly altered. In a study of fifty dreams (Epstein, 1988), eighteen dream images were not identical to the waking event.

The dream image is slightly altered but unequivocally associated. The alteration enlarges a category by the addition of an associated item. The categories, above, are blond woman, Indian physician of the nervous system, leg deformity and two boys, respectively.

The same phenomenon is present in Freud's dreams (1900) that he reported to show dream dependence on waking events.

The categories are plant monograph, beneficent organization, and island, respectively.

Why is the waking event not merely reproduced in these instances but transformed, usually minimally, into a related image? An obligatory process is at work (Epstein, 1988); a process designed to form new associative connections, thus increasing associated items within categories; therefore, enlarging categories.

Waking Event	Dream Image
Monograph on genus Cyclamen	Monograph on a certain species of plant
Communications received from Liberal Election Committee and from Council of the Humanitarian League	Communication from the Social Democratic Committee
Thought of Dreyfus on the Ile du Diable	A man standing on a cliff in the middle of the sea

In the instance of a "man with amputation below knee" becoming, in the dream, a "woman with bifid leg below knee," a new item has been fit into the category of leg deformity. This transformation of the waking event is a step in the building of a category which eventually, as discussed in "Aphasia," chapter 2, and in "Epilepsy," chapter 3, is presumed to occupy a specific neuronal locus.

Ictal discharge of the underlying locus (neuronal network) brings into consciousness the category contents, as in Kubie's (1953) case cited in chapter 3 where items appearing ictally were in the category of "someone wresting something from someone's grasp." Theoretically, should there be ictal discharge of the neuronal network underlying the leg deformity category, which is formed in part by processing of the dream's day residue, images entering consciousness would be "a man with an amputation below the knee" and "a woman with a bifid leg below the knee."

Varied functions then are served by the brain's activity in converting a waking event into a dream image. These include: matching of very recent with earlier memories; serving as a vehicle for discharge of affectively laden conations; increasing associative connectivity and strength; increasing the information store by forming and enlarging categorical structures.

Observations on the role of memory processing and of category building in dreams may be summarized as follows:

1. Childhood memories, because of their synaptic strength and dominance, enter adult dreams.
2. Processing of current memories is a survival essential as is their matching with earlier memories. In matching, the two become associatively linked, joined in categories.
3. Déjà vu is viewed as the linking of an immediate perceived event with an already embedded memory as occurs in waking event/dream image processing. The processing mechanism becomes unmasked in the milieu of dysregulation produced by temporolimbic discharge.
4. Waking event/dream image processing is a cyclic brain event. The method of selection of a given waking event for dream incorporation is unsolved.
5. Waking event/dream image processing has varied functions including the matching of very recent with earlier memories and the formation of associative connections, leading to enlargement of categorical structures.

9

The Normative Dream

The dream is one of nature's supreme creations. Likely originating in prehuman mentation, a preverbal imagistic thought, meeting such survival necessities as memory processing, learning with its category building, and the release of instinctual energies, the dream continued to evolve with the appearance of *Homo sapiens*, adding to its repertoire words and their elaboration into the complexities of language. The images and words of dreaming spin out of the brain's cyclic activity.

As noted, varied functions have been increasingly assigned to the dream from the wish fulfillment sleep preserving of Freud, the homeostatic compensatory of Jung, the problem-solving information building and memory processing of later students. As is true of all biologic systems, many functions are condensed into one system.

Dream mechanisms were comprehensively described by Freud (1900). What are some mechanisms employed in the formation of the normative dream? The day residue is a nidus for the elaboration of dream imagery (chapter 8). Release of inhibition over associative processes permits very active associative activity. There is rapid immediate connectivity so that one associative item becomes coupled to another as equivalents (displacement), or several items become connected by condensation and are embraced by an overarching structure: a symbol.

As a result of associative release, memories of every type, ontogenetic and possibly phylogenetic, become accessible (chapters 7 and 8). The dream milieu also permits loosening of inhibition over affects with resultant heightened or vivid emotionality. Despite the appearance of vivid emotionality, a modulating force operates in the dream preventing the appearance of material too archaic or catastrophic. Although there is usually suspension of logic (the secondary process), thought is present and serves to shape the dream narrative. This is called secondary revision. Some of these functions and mechanisms are displayed in normative (personal unpublished) dreams.

> Dream 1: I am the quarterback. I speak to X (the coach of a local professional team). I line up. Aggressively. I call the first play. I decide to start off with a run. It's a good first play—to test the other team. The ball goes to the running back. Makes a few yards. Ms. Y (head nurse) is in the huddle. I decide to go to a short pass. Someone suggests it. We make a considerable gain. Not sure it's a first down. Will try another pass. I'm shouting a string of numbers as we line up. I'm off to the side. Not in the "T" position. I call off numbers. How will the center know when to pass the ball back? Then I see a big obstruction—green—a huge hedge. I'm glad I'm the quarterback.

Day Residue

About thirty hours before the dream, I read that our local football team had acquired a new quarterback and center; the coach's name was also mentioned in the news account. About fifteen hours before the dream, my retirement from the faculty was mentioned at a meeting attended by a head nurse.

Connectivity

The mechanism of identification, fusion of the self with the team and new quarterback, is clear. Identification is an internalization; here a form of displacement from the actual quarterback to the self.

Condensation of associative items across categories is likely albeit speculative. A "pass" is a football play but also a sexual assertion. "Shouting numbers" is a quarterback's duty but also evokes the passage of years. "Off to the side" is not the quarterback's usual playing position but is also a shift in status. "Hedge" is in a botanical category but semantically, a preservation of options, not taking unequivocal action.

MOTIVATIONAL FORCES

Somewhat weakened by mention of retirement and perhaps other factors, masculine self-esteem is restored by aggressively leading a professional football team. Elements of wish fulfillment and problem solving are thus present. A perfect solution of the problem may not be forthcoming, illustrated by the appearance of a huge obstructive hedge.

MODULATION

The dream is well modulated. Feeling tone is pleasant. Only once is the fear mechanism released from inhibition: "How will the center know when to pass it back?"

SECONDARY REVISION

The dream narrative flows quickly. Sequencing and accuracy are of high order and virtually reproduce the actual play-calling of a quarterback. Therefore, the secondary revision is close to waking thought. Such proximity to waking thought is considered the level of the "preconscious."

> Dream 2: X is massaging a man's back. It seemed too sexually explicit. Then she left. A woman was looking for her. A nurse supervisor. X was supposed to be at an assignment but she wasn't. The woman said, "Well, we'll get F. E."

DAY RESIDUE

I had coffee with X, a woman of high attraction, about seventeen hours before the dream. She spoke of the need to gain independence particularly from remnants of concern over her parents' disapproval.

CONNECTIVITY

There is displacement from self to "a man." The "nurse supervisor," an item in the category of "female parental figure," arises from the day residue. Note "mother" is not directly represented but is slightly altered into "nurse supervisor," an unequivocally associated item (chapter 8). F. E. (the initials of my sister's name) also keenly values independence. X and F. E. are associated within the category of strong independent women. Also, by association, sexual interest toward sister is implied.

MOTIVATIONAL FORCES

The erotic attraction to X gains wish-fulfillment despite its displacement from the self. By association, sexual interest toward sister is implied.

MODULATION

The dream is well modulated with no painful affect. Feeling tone is pleasant. Childhood sexual strivings toward sister are not overt; they undergo inhibition.

SECONDARY REVISION

The narrative flows smoothly although more sparsely than in Dream 1; the material also seems more removed from the level of preconscious ideation. The naming of F. E., a movement away from X, although both are in the same category, represents the obligatory associative process. This particular obligatory association may come either from "below," a product of instant "reflex" associative connection, or from "above," a guiding of thought, a joining of semantic equals, by the more synthetic activity of secondary revision.

> Dream 3: A departmental group. X, Y, and me. Y had done something wrong. We had to descend to some subterranean room. Walk down about three to four flights. Into a room where we were locked in. We had to raise our arms and shout in unison, under X's (a supervisor) direction. A sense of coercion. A punishment. A disturbing feeling tone.

DAY RESIDUE

About fifteen hours before the dream, a hotel down escalator stopped running. I had to walk down the escalator as if it were a staircase. It seemed odd, and another person commented on it.

CONNECTIVITY

The down escalator of the day residue is associatively connected to, not the identical, but unequivocally related association, "walked down about three to four flights." The image of "walked down" gathers up connections; it becomes a condensation connected to the semantic categories of descent, a descent to the lower depths, the subterranean, the underworld, Hades, Hell—all sites of punishment. "Locked in" is linked to jail, another site of punishment. The dreamer's sense of guilt is projected onto Y; an identification of projective type, a displacement.

MOTIVATIONAL FORCES

The initial departmental setting suggests collegiality but, ambivalently, a struggle for power. The struggle ends in a defeat, reduction to regimentation, punishment. This outcome produces the painful feeling tone associated with humiliation and shame. Self-esteem is reduced.

MODULATION

Modulation fails in this dream because of the emergence of dysphoria, accompanying brutal and despairing images. This imagery and painful feeling tone have an uncanny quality as may be encountered in certain waking psychotic states.

SECONDARY REVISION

The narrative is congruent with the feeling tone. Does the narrative stem from the day residue of "walking down" with elaboration into the guilt motif; or is it derived from a "higher" organizing force exploring a guilt theme? Likely, there is interplay between the two; interplay between crude association and narrative organization.

> Dream 4: On a huge plane traveling to London. Very pleased I am going there. With family. Wandering about the interesting plane. The plane has landed—but it is in water. I see a skyline ahead—that must be London. There are tugboats around the plane. They're there to dock the plane. Then we arrive at a hotel in London. I feel expectant, happy. I'm wanting to walk about and see London. I'm with wife and family in the hotel room. Only two of the four children there. Where will the children sleep? Then I see there is an extra bed. Is it big enough to hold the children?

DAY RESIDUE

About fifteen hours before the dream, a barber whom I had known for many years interrupted his retirement to do temporary work. He spoke with great pleasure about the joys of retirement, particularly of a week's Caribbean cruise. He described the luxuries of the ship and the beautiful waters.

About eight hours before the dream, I was talking, in the company of my two sons, to a married pregnant woman, a friend of my son, who had just discovered she was carrying twins. She showed, to all, an ultrasound intrauterine picture of the two. About forty hours before the dream, I was talking with interest to a Swedish colleague about general weather conditions in Stockholm. About twenty-one hours before the dream, I was reading about the dangerous turbulence produced by the wakes of very large planes. Other relatively recent waking events which fall outside day residue time limits and which are more probably recent but established memories, also influenced the dream material. About eleven days before the dream, I returned on a large plane (a Boeing 767) from Philadelphia and was struck by its size. Previously, on arriving in Philadelphia, I commented on the skyline observable on the drive from the airport.

About six months before the dream, I traveled by small boat across the wide expanse of Manila Bay. Also about six months before, while on a small boat on another Philippine body of water, dangerous conditions arose due to a storm. There was concern about safe arrival.

CONNECTIVITY

In a dream of this type, one association may lead to another in a voluminous stream. The barber's comment about the joys of the cruise ship is matched with the image of travel by plane. Both are in the same category: instruments of transportation. The plane image is modified; it becomes more like a ship—it lands on water and has attending tugboats. This seaplane condenses ship and plane.

The ship and its modified image connect with the earlier memory of traveling across Manila Bay as well as the hazardous Philippines boat journey. The London plane image is connected to the Philadelphia plane. The planes are linked by identity. London and Philadelphia are items in the category of large cities. Both have skylines. Stockholm is also an item in this category. The two unborn children become connected to my two children, not the actual four; although now adults, the two are pictured as children. Is the hotel bed, associatively linked to the womb, an item in the category of enclosures containing humans? Is the bed big enough to hold the two?

MOTIVATIONAL FORCES

The dream fulfills a long-standing wish to visit and explore London. This is also a wish for novelty and adventure—openness as compared to the subterranean room of dream 3 (which occurred on a different day, as did all these dreams). London symbolizes a new life as does the pregnant womb. This may be more meaningful to an older individual; a wish to regain an earlier period of life symbolized by only two offspring, both pictured as children—as in earlier days.

MODULATION

The dream, accompanied by pleasant affect, is well modulated. The uneventful landing of the plane on water may be "healing over" the anxiety of capsizing in the Philippines waters. No direct dream of this incident has occurred—suggesting the general modulating function of the dream in its processing of traumatic, but not reaching the catastrophic, waking episodes.

SECONDARY REVISION

The dream is well sequenced with a strong element of pleasurable expectancy. The narrative unfolds in an orderly fashion.

ASPECTS OF MODULATION
AND SECONDARY REVISION

Modulation is a homeostatic activity, a balancing of pleasurable and painful feeling tones. At the neuronal level, such balancing operates through excitatory and inhibitory forces. These forces attenuate painful feeling tone, for fearful ideation and imagery is common in dreams. The emergence of painful emotions must be diluted. This was recognized by Freud (1900); the dream is the "guardian of sleep" operating through censorship, a homeostatic force regulating the intensity of connectivity and its associated affects.

Modulation is a less anthropomorphic term than *censorship*. Modulation operates in all biologic systems of the organism. In neuronal terms, modulatory activity may occur between cells of neuronal networks, between networks themselves, or via pathways from higher regulatory centers.

Modulation acts not only at the interface between dream and waking states, the level of the preconscious, but also within deeper levels of the unconscious. There are repressive barriers (modulating forces) between deeper (archaic) levels of the unconscious and more recently evolved layers; such barriers prevent overly arousing or catastrophic material from entering dream awareness.

Secondary revision and modulation work hand-in-hand. Secondary revision also interdigitates with the "primary" mechanisms of pure connectivity: displacement and condensation. Freud considered secondary revision a product of preconscious activity. The preconscious abuts on waking consciousness; secondary revision is very closely related to waking thought.

It is an object of wonder that secondary revision, as it unreels the dream scenario in sequence and in great detail, is involuntary. The scenario is occurring without conscious volition and control. Secondary revision indicates the mind's capacity to involuntarily form a vast assemblage of consistent mentation. Such a capacity must be a product of higher brain centers; participation of prefrontal and other advanced areas. The phenomenon of secondary revision suggests there is involuntary flowing ideation while awake (preconscious), playing a role in problem solving and in the creation of new thought structures (Strunz, 1993).

DREAM ANALYSIS

Dream analysis is concerned with the motivational, the conative, forces operating upon connectivity and imaginal processes to form the dream. Wish fulfillment, postulated by Freud, and problem solving are key. Motivation is powered by pleasure seeking and pain avoidance, although the two may be intermixed. Both wish fulfillment and problem solving guide the ego–self system in its search to maximize pleasure and reduce pain. Dream analysis must consider these motivational forces and their underpinnings.

Observations on the normative dream may be summarized as follows:

1. The normative dream may be understood in terms of: day residue, connectivity, motivational forces, modulation, and secondary revision.
2. Condensation of associated items and symbol structure are intimately related.
3. Wish fulfillment and problem solving are key motivational forces generating the dream.
4. Modulation is a homeostatic activity operating at the dream–waking interface. Modulation also establishes repressive barriers at various levels of the deeper unconscious.
5. Secondary revision is closely related to waking thought but is a completely involuntary process.

10

Two Types of Dream Pathology

Every biological system is subject to pathologic alteration. Knowledge of disordered structure or function sheds light on the nature of the intact system. Certain disorders affect dreaming although the study of dream pathology is embryonic. There are two broad types of dream pathology: a deficit type with loss or paucity of dreaming; a positive type with ample, overly vivid dreaming. The former involves dream components of connectivity and secondary revision; the latter, modulation.

IMPAIRED CONNECTIVITY AND SECONDARY REVISION

Fundamental "reflex" connectivity requires an intact cerebral cortex in terms of cell assemblies and neurotransmitters. Influence of subcortical centers is also assumed. Processes of secondary revision and associative connectivity are intimately related. Secondary revision makes use of the associative items presented, but, as a more developed function, may initiate specific associative flows. Associative activity with its displacements, condensations, and formation of new items depends upon semantic and phonemic relationships. Not only is the auditory mode essential but the visual (and other modalities as well) since this is the dream's chief mode of expression. Any process affecting

91

the neuronal substrate of imagery or of language proper should alter normative dreaming. Cessation of dreaming, for example, was reported by Humphrey and Zangwill (1951) after parieto-occipital (visual area) injury and by others (vide infra) after midleft hemispheric (language area) lesions.

APHASIA AND DREAMING

Chapter 2 demonstrated that connectivity processes are impaired in aphasia, particularly the fluidity of connectivity as manifested by the tenacious binding of associative items. The rapid darting nature of ongoing connectivity in the dream is thus rendered impossible. Whether or not an impairment in associative processes is the only factor, loss of dreaming does occur in some aphasias.

Foulkes (1978) noted cessation of dreaming in two individuals aphasic as a consequence of cerebrovascular disease. Stoller (1980), in his obituary of a noted American psychoanalyst, observed that aphasia following a cerebral embolus was accompanied, in this physician, by cessation of dreaming. Later, dreaming returned and with it significant recovery from the aphasia. Epstein and Simmons (1983) reported loss of dreaming in seven individuals, aphasic due to acute midleft hemispheric vascular lesions.

Clearly, more study of the language–dreaming relationship and of that between aphasia recovery and dreaming return is required. Indeed, Greenberg and Dewan (1969) studied all-night sleep in fifteen aphasic individuals and found a correlation between aphasia improvement and higher percentages of REM sleep; suggesting the greater amount of REM was mirroring a "reprogramming" process in the brain.

Loss of dreaming with subsequent return accompanying language improvement was noted in a 35-year-old woman rendered aphasic by a midleft hemispheric lesion (embolization) (Epstein and Simmons, 1983). With aphasia onset, the patient reported loss of dreaming, which persisted for four months. Six months after onset, she reported two dreams:

> Dream 1: I was doing arithmetic in school in the ninth grade class. I can't remember anything else. The teacher was there. It wasn't the teacher in the ninth grade class. I don't even know who she was.

DAY RESIDUE

On the dream day the patient had been working on arithmetic problems as part of her rehabilitation program.

CONNECTIVITY

The ninth grade is "where I did algebra and algebra gave me trouble." This is connected to her current stroke-related difficulties in arithmetic. She could not describe the teacher although this image is connected to the speech therapist who is not represented identically but is unequivocally associated.

MOTIVATIONAL FORCES

These are not clearly expressed.

MODULATION

The dream is well modulated.

SECONDARY REVISION

The content is restricted with no elaboration or sequencing.

> Dream 2: My kid was playing with a ball.

DAY RESIDUE

On the dream day, the patient's son was playing with a beanbag.

CONNECTIVITY

The son is directly represented. Other associative linkages are not apparent although there may be identification with the son.

MOTIVATIONAL FORCES

The patient is expressing a wish for increased manual dexterity.

MODULATION

The dream is well modulated.

SECONDARY REVISION

The patient said, "This is a real short dream—he was just playing and just holding a ball." The dream is indeed constricted without elaboration and sequencing but simply reproducing a daily event. Thus, secondary revision is impaired.

About six-and-one-half months after onset, another dream was reported.

> Dream 3: I was sitting at the table—sitting here—could see myself over here. I was doing something. I was playing cards. Some sort of game. Someone woke me up after that.

DAY RESIDUE

The patient had been playing solitaire. She frequently handles cards as part of her therapy.

CONNECTIVITY

There is virtually no active connectivity.

MOTIVATIONAL FORCES

These are not clearly expressed.

MODULATION

The dream is well modulated.

SECONDARY REVISION

A daily event is simply reproduced with no additional sequencing or elaboration. Secondary revision is therefore impaired.

Dreams continued in this fashion with restricted content, little elaboration beyond the day residue and vagueness in remembering content, until seven-and-one-half months after onset when she reported a dream moving beyond the day residue with increased connectivity, stronger secondary revision, and containing an element of anxiety—related to the open-heart procedure with its subsequent embolization and aphasia.

> Dream 4: I was in the hospital. I was supposed to be in surgery. One of the doctors—she said, "You have to go to surgery." I said, "No." They took me anyway. Then there was a man doctor, a surgeon. The woman doctor was somewhere behind me. She was the one who talked to me. Just about the time the anesthetist would let you go out—that's when I woke up.

Accompanying the return of increased connectivity and stronger secondary revision, the aphasia improved. Although some subsequent dreams lacked density, the positive movement in both dreams and aphasia continued and, ten-and-one-half months after onset, the patient could report this dream:

> Dream 5: I was looking for a job at Michoud. That's not where I used to work. It was in a huge, huge hanger. Going into there to look for a job. I always thought they ought to have pictures in the hanger—to look for a job—pictures of TV telling about astronauts and stuff in space.

Beautiful. And I suggested this. When I went in there, it wasn't there and I looked at it and a little boy and husband looked at it and he undid everything and I had to reset the whole thing to get it all and could see astronauts clearly and it was in color. Blue sky and white space suits. Saw a rocket going up with fire coming out.

It would seem that damage to networks resulting in aphasia also impairs dreaming, particularly processes of connectivity, secondary revision, and affect inclusion. Improvement in both waking language and dream follows a parallel course.

IMPAIRED MODULATION

Impaired modulation seems the most frequent dream pathology. Recurrence, stereotypy, and unbridled fear are characteristic of impaired modulation and have been discussed in the dreams of posttraumatic stress disorder (chapter 4), in recurrent dream–epilepsy equivalence (chapters 5 and 6), and in typical dream phenomena (chapter 7). Another product of impaired modulation are the disturbing dreams of narcolepsy.

NARCOLEPSY

Narcoleptic dream phenomena have clear physiological correlates as has been revealed with the advent of all-night sleep studies (Dement and Kleitman, 1957). In general, all-night sleep studies have established the correlation of REM sleep with dreaming; the cyclic appearance of REM periods during the night's sleep; the percentage of the night's sleep occupied by REM; the time of onset of the night's first REM period (REM latency); the presence of muscle atonia during the REM period; and varied physiological changes during REM including penile erection.

Narcolepsy's chief characteristic is the sudden sleep attack. Other features of the narcoleptic tetrad are cataplexy, sudden loss of muscle tone often accompanying emotional excitement; hypnagogic hallucinations, vivid visual imagery at transitions of waking and sleep states; and sleep paralysis, body immobilization usually at sleep–waking transitions. In addition, frightening dreams during nocturnal sleep often occur (Daniels, 1934; Brock and Wiesel, 1941).

A 51-year-old man (personal unpublished case) with narcolepsy, cataplexy, and sleep paralysis reported disturbing catastrophic dreams during the night's sleep.

Dream 6: I was in a meat packing place. I was a supervisor. I got caught up in a machine and one of my arms went one way and a leg went the other.

Lack of modulation permits the appearance of marked fear and imagery of body disintegration. This theme is recurrent with this individual.

Dream 7: Someone is coming in to chop my head off with an ax.

One terrifying dream was accompanied by sleep paralysis.

Dream 8: Someone breaking into the house and hurting family.

Daniels (1934), studying 147 cases, found "the nocturnal dreams of narcoleptic patients are generally either terrifying, or at least distinctly unpleasant" (p. 32).

Dream 9 (Daniels, 1934): "Dreamed of snakes and monsters, of being chased by wild animals, of lying on an infant and being unable to move" [p. 32].

In another individual, impaired modulation permitted the appearance of grotesque body imagery.

Dream 10 (Daniels, 1934): "Cats were coming out of her mouth" [p. 32].

Dreams described by Daniels in narcoleptics are "typical" in their themes of being chased and of the self-endangered.
Brock and Wiesel (1941) described frightening dreams in a narcoleptic individual.

Dream 11: "Large animals appeared, viz, elephants as big as a house. Later smaller animals, such as squirrels and rats, appeared" [p. 705].

In the same individual:

Dream 12: "A male voice would say, 'I am going to scalp you'" [p. 705].

Daniels (1934) differentiated hypnagogic hallucinations accompanied by cataplexy and/or sleep paralysis from dreams occurring in the midst of sleep, although these hallucinations are now considered REM phenomena, that is, products of the dream mechanism. Hypnagogic hallucinations "often have reference to animals, particularly those of which the appearance usually excites revulsion" (p. 21).

Dream 13 (Daniels, 1934) associated with body immobility: "Forms appeared at the windows and entered the room; she often felt as though snakes, birds and other creatures were moving about in her abdomen and coming out of her mouth. She frequently dreamed that operations were being performed on her" [p. 23].

Daniels cites a case of hypnagogic imagery associated with an inability to move, containing archaic uncanny imagery.

Dream 14: Troupes of women who seemed to swarm about his bed and try to choke him.

Other archaic images in dream states accompanied by cataplexy, cited by Daniels, are: "a snake was biting him"; "a rat crawling out through his skin"; "a brightly colored parrot that called him names."

All-night sleep studies have clarified the nature of narcolepsy. Dement, Rechtschaffen, and Gulevich (1966) demonstrated a virtual immediate onset of REM sleep in neuroleptics as compared to the normal latency. Sleep onset REM was identified by usual criteria: the characteristic electroencephalogram, rapid eye movements on the electrooculogram, and atonia on the electromyogram. The narcoleptic attacks themselves displayed full characteristics of REM sleep including absence of tonic electromyographic potentials. Therefore, the sleep attack of narcolepsy is a REM episode. Further, the other components of the narcoleptic tetrad are also manifestations of the REM process. Cataplexy and sleep paralysis are manifestations of REM atonia. The vivid and terrifying nature of hypnagogic hallucinations must also be considered a reflection of a disordered REM mechanism leading to failure of dream modulation.

REM SLEEP BEHAVIOR DISORDER

If atonia were not present during the REM period, it would theoretically be possible to enact a dream, to respond to dream images. Such a possibility, however, could not be fully realized until the delineation of REM sleep behavior disorder (Schenck, Bundlie, and Mahowald, 1985). In the small number of cases collected, etiology appears related to brain disease, particularly lesions in the tegmentum of pons and mesencephalon (Culebras and Moore, 1989) affecting nuclei and descending tracts normally inhibiting spinal motor centers. Destruction of inhibitory pathways permits tonic muscle activity and capacity for movement.

Nature has thus opened a new window on the dream; the opportunity to observe enactment of a dream. In cases of REM sleep behavior disorder where dreams are reported, content is poorly modulated, contains archaic imagery, and is accompanied by varied complex movements.

One individual (Culebras and Moore, 1989), aged 70, who dreamed "an alligator was trying to get into his car" and he was holding "the animal's snout with great force" found himself grabbing his wife's arm upon awakening. In another dream a bear was chasing him, "he threw something at the animal, which turned out to be the bedcovers."

Schenck, Hurwitz, and Mahowald (1988) described a 67-year-old man who "would jump out of bed and throw punches while dreaming of being attacked by animals or unfamiliar people." Once, the patient put his wife's "head in an arm lock and punched her repeatedly while he was dreaming" (p. 652).

These vivid terrifying dreams are similar to those of the narcoleptic. They have a life-threatening "typical" quality. Imagery, with its frequent animal content, is archaic. In common with narcolepsy, REM sleep behavior disorder represents a disturbance in the REM mechanism. This disturbance must contribute to the faulty modulation of the dream content itself. The content does not seem subserved by a specific dominant network but rather by the release of networks, highly charged, normally inhibited, but potentially dominant.

The material on dream pathology may be summarized as follows:

1. There are two broad types of dream pathology: the deficit and the recurrent, overly vivid.
2. The former displays impairment of connectivity and secondary revision; the latter of modulation.
3. The deficit type is found in certain aphasias.

4. Additional etiologies of impaired modulation, besides those described previously, include two REM mechanism disturbances: narcolepsy and REM sleep behavior disorder.
5. The loss of or constriction of dreaming encountered in certain aphasias may improve parallel to aphasia improvement.
6. A characteristic of impaired modulation, in the REM mechanism disturbances, is frightening and archaic dream imagery.

11

Levels of the Unconscious

As noted, failure of dream modulation permits the appearance of archaic imagery. This suggests levels of the unconscious exist and that "deeper" levels do not ordinarily have access to dream awareness except under certain conditions. The unconscious may be defined as mental activity not reporting to waking awareness (Rado, 1949). Associative linking and network consolidation, for example, may be in continuous activity but are in the unconscious domain, since they do not report to awareness.

Mental activity reporting to dream awareness, however, is unconscious in origin since it appears involuntarily and in a new and unexpected guise. Although reporting to dream awareness, the dream itself is formed by the unconscious. Not only is the dream the "royal road to the unconscious," but it is the unconscious.

At what may be taken as the "shallow" level of the unconscious (the preconscious) is mentation almost immediately available to awareness. Fantasy (imaginative mental play) is an example. Fantasy draws upon unconscious sources, but the material is voluntarily directed and has limits in terms of the depth attained. Automatized mentation, affectively neutral memories, and dream content of a pedestrian nature are further examples of "shallow" level activity. At deeper, not as accessible, levels lies imagery or mentation subject to active inhibition (repression). Such inhibition is a modulatory (homeostatic) force exerted to prevent overly painful mentation or imagery from entering dreaming awareness. Material thus repressed includes memories, old, and perhaps relatively recent, encoded with painful feeling tone; encoding of early childhood events with their accompaniments of novelty, vividness, pleasure, or fearful threat; speculatively, phylogenetic encodings with their wordless uncanny vividness. There are layers of repressive barriers operative on unconscious material; the deepest barrier preventing archaic products from gaining access to dream awareness.

RUPTURE OF REPRESSIVE BARRIERS

Failure of modulation as encountered in the recurrent dreams of temporolimbic epilepsy, in typical dreams, in the hypnagogic hallucinations and midnocturnal dreams of narcolepsy, permit archaic imagery to come to dream, then waking awareness. The modulatory failure may be attributed to dominant circuits overcoming inhibitory mechanisms or to primary weakening of inhibition (repression) itself.

In general, the mentation or imagery released is concerned with threats to survival, to body integrity; it has a primitive archaic quality. Not only survival is threatened, but the body is mutilated, the individual tortured. The feared object is human or an animal with repellent qualities.

This mentation-imagery is ordinarily repressed because of its devastating impact on mental homeostasis. Not only does repression fail in the epileptic, epileptoid, and REM mechanism derangements cited, but may also do so when network activity is affected by metabolic change (delirium tremens) or by chemicals such as LSD (Grof, 1985), levodopa (Nausieda, Weiner, Kaplan, Weber, and Klawans, 1982), or adverse effects of thiothixene (Solomon, 1983).

Solomon's three cases in which painful archaic dreams occurred following thiothixene administration are of interest because of the identity of imagery in three disparate individuals suggesting a transpersonal factor, a species pre-disposition.

In Case 1, a woman "was awakened several times by very frightening and vivid nightmares. In these nightmares, she and her family and friends were being tortured and muti-lated" (p. 77).

In Case 2, a woman "reported awakening two or three times a night from vivid nightmares in which she and family members were being tortured" (p. 77).

In Case 3, a woman was awakened several times during the night by vivid dreams which "involved torture and muti-lation of faceless individuals" (p. 77). In all three cases, the dysphoric dreams were never previously experienced, were recurrent, and ceased upon discontinuation of thiothixene.

In Solomon's cases, one assumes an alteration in neuro-transmission, its specific nature unknown. The alteration affects network function either by weakening inhibitory networks or by causing excessive discharge of networks lying at "deep" levels of the unconscious subserving transpersonal imagery.

It is unlikely these three individuals actually experienced mutilation and torture. They may, however, have witnessed such scenes, for example, in the cinema; their memory so repellent that they were repressed. Overly strong repression may create a potential dysequilibrium with a tendency for the repressive barrier to become dislodged. The transpersonal nature of the imagery suggests a species characteristic, per-haps genetically determined in the sense of Jung's (1953) collective unconscious.

Just as there may be a superimposition of recent and old memories, so there may be a superimposition of one level of the unconscious on another, a "shallower" level with a "deeper" one, as though there is a push for expression from the deep, more archaic levels, a push against the hypertro-phied strength of the repressive barriers. Not only do deeper networks make their appearance, along with the shallow, in dreams, but they may be employed as expressions of current waking conflicts. In a case of Bartemeier's (1950), "a young woman dreamed that her girlfriend had been murdered and that she and her mother were dismembering the corpse and packing the parts into a trunk to conceal the crime. They were in a great hurry because of their fear of detection by the police" (p. 10).

Shortly after this dream, the patient entered a state of "agitated depression," testifying to the occasional ill consequences of rupture of repressive barriers. Bartemeier shows the dream expressed hatred toward the girlfriend because the dreamer's mother "manifested a preference for her"; further, "this activated the dreamer's infantile situation with her mother and younger sister" (p. 10). Archaic mutilation imagery became available to express a current conflict; networks subserving such imagery, pushing for expression, are able in these instances to rupture the repressive barrier.

ANIMAL IMAGERY

Animals, as living things, fit a specific category (chapter 2). They carry significant affective weight in the human mind and appear uncanny. Through human history, particularly during earlier phases when they abounded in close proximity to humans, animals condensed various meanings and emotions: fear, admiration, envy, worship, guilt. These emotions led to identification with animals: the wearing of animal masks, the establishment of totemic groups. Animals are not completely responsive to human control. The potential of attack persists: the bite of snake, dog, horse; the bite and invasive burrowing of the rat.

Children are particularly responsive to animals as evidenced by frequent animal images in their dreams and in beloved or feared fairy tales. Fascination and fear coalesce. The child is small and fears destruction by the huge animal. Memories of such childhood arousal require later repression to preserve homeostasis. These likely hypertrophied repressive barriers may be dislodged in later life as when modulation is impaired in the REM mechanism disorders (chapter 10). From the deep unconscious, one dreams of being chased by wild animals (dream 9); of cats, snakes, birds entering the body (dreams 10 and 13); of a rat having entered, crawling out from the body. No longer repressed are fears of actual combat with a threatening animal as in the REM sleep behavior disorder.

In animal dreams, the most intense human fears are realized. Throughout human history, how many attacks by animals have occurred; how many struggles to the death; how many memories of these encounters have been preserved and perhaps transmitted? How many of these catastrophic encounters, also joyful identifications, have found their place in neuronal networks? If the mind of the child is most open to phylogenetic impresses, the animal phobias of childhood may confirm these speculations.

In Freud's case of Little Hans (1909a), a 5-year-old boy feared a horse would bite him in the street, and he avoided such encounters. At the zoo, he refused to visit the giraffe or elephant. Horse, giraffe, and elephant are in the category of large animals. Fear is attached to each of these associated items. In Freud's view, the fear more properly should attach to Hans' father (also in the category of "large" organisms) because here the fundamental anxiety exists. An associative connection is made between horse and father. The fear, Freud indicates, is displaced from its true source, the father, to the horse. This may be the case, but a child responds vividly to animals, generating animal imagery in dreams. The primary object of the child's fear would more reasonably be the horse springing, as it does, from the matrix of phylogenetically determined feared animals. The horse generates fear in Hans, a fear that would exist outside the pale of the castration complex; a fear that could be secondarily displaced by associative connectivity to the father. When Hans was seen at age 19, no longer a child, the horse phobia had disappeared.

Animal phobias in a 2-year-old were reported by Sperling (1952). This child would "wake up nightly and scream in fear, 'a doggy is biting my finger,' 'a kitty is biting my finger,' or 'a fish is biting my finger'" (p. 116). She would also scream out in sleep itself. The child was "afraid to go out into the street for fear that she might see a dog or cat" (pp. 116–117). Again, the animal images are not considered by the author as the primary vessels of fear but rather as displacements from the "true" feared object, for example, the mother, or as foci for the projection of the child's own aggressive impulses to bite. The animal image is a symbol, that is, it has the capacity to condense varied strivings but, again, animals evoke fear simply by their presence.

THE NATURE OF DREAMING: ANIMAL AND HUMAN

Ingenious experiments with cats employ severance of descending pontine tegmental pathways, thus removing inhibition on spinal motor neurons in REM sleep, permitting tonic and phasic motor activity (Sastre and Jouvet, 1979; Hendricks, Morrison, and Mann, 1982). This is analogous to the pontine lesions described in human REM behavior disorder.

It has always been assumed that animals, at least mammals, dream as evidenced by their easily observed extremity and eye movements during sleep. Indeed, REM sleep has been demonstrated through the animal kingdom. That animals do dream seems further confirmed by the experiments cited since varied behaviors are enacted during REM sleep.

These enactments are reminiscent of attacks on objects with intermittent periods of quiet staring or searching (head orienting) movements; also, simple locomotion occurs. Interestingly, the enactments observed by these two independent groups of experimenters are virtually identical except that the earlier work of Sastre and Jouvet also demonstrated postures of fear, rage, and licking. The type of behavior demonstrated appears to depend on pontine lesion sites (Hendrick et al., 1982).

One may surmise that the cat dreams, at least in part, of objects of prey and of attacking these objects; of surveying its environment in a posture of vigilance. Such dreams having survival value are potentially genetically programmed; and possibly analogous, at least the dream of vigilance, to the human typical dream of the "object endangered." Perhaps the cat in its dreams experiences the emotions of rage and of fear.

Likely, the frequent occurrence of anxiety or fear, not catastrophic but sufficiently disturbing, in human dreams has adaptive value, phylogenetically determined, increasing alertness to environmental threats rather than solely reflecting daily problems. In this connection, the strong prevalence of human nightmares and their independence from daytime anxiety has been noted by Wood and Bootzin (1990). The dream world is, in large part, a world of danger, of anticipation of danger; helping to master the external world in the service of survival. One is reminded of the prevalence of fearful as opposed to pleasurable emotion in human temporolimbic epilepsy (chapter 3)—confirmation of the evolutionary survival value of fear.

The work of Sastre and Jouvet; of Hendricks, Morrison, and Mann throws light on the enigma of animal dreaming. What, can we speculate, are the characteristics of feline dreaming?

FELINE DREAMING

1. Waking event enters dream (day residue).
2. Day residue is compared to earlier memories.
3. Memory bank is enlarged and strengthened.
4. Obligatory associations are formed.
5. Associated items are automatically categorized.

6. Categorical structures are enlarged.
7. Imagery has survival value:
     Searching and vigilance
     Predation (approach)
     Fear (avoidance)
     Rage (defense)
8. Blocked instinctual needs are consummated.

Such dreams may represent the fundamental mammalian pattern; the fundamental deep layers of the human unconscious.

With increasing complexity of the mammalian brain through the primate order, with its hierarchical social life, up to the human level with its language acquisition and complex ego–self system, additional features are superimposed.

SUPERIMPOSED FEATURES IN HUMAN DREAMING

1. Elaborate secondary revision.
2. Symbolic representation with powerful condensation capacity.
3. Increased displacement capacity powered by internalizing (identification) and externalizing (projective) mechanisms.
4. Complex ego–self system representation:
     Maintenance of self-esteem
     Resolution of drive-conscience conflicts
5. Increased memory storage:
     Retention of very early memories
     Retention of species memories as products of long and
        complex cultural history

The material on levels of the unconscious may be summarized as follows:

1. Failure of inhibition (repression) releases deep layers of the unconscious as manifested by vivid archaic dream imagery.
2. The vivid archaic imagery relates to survival fears particularly threats to body integrity; also employs animal images with roots in childhood, and likely in human phylogeny.
3. Archaic imagery is always potentially available.
4. Neurophysiological experimentation on cats permitting "enactment" of dreams sheds light on the nature of feline dreaming, in turn, on fundamental levels of human dreaming, that is, on deep levels of the human unconscious. Profound complexities have been erected on this base in the human.

12

Dominant Networks: Imperative Fetishistic and Phobic Ideas

As defined by Webster, an idea is "a representation or construct of memory and association as distinguished from direct impression of sense." The role of memory in providing the raw material for an idea, and of association in building an idea's structure, is evident. Ideas may be formed at an abstract level, but this does not negate the influence of memory and association. However abstract the idea, it has an internal cerebral substratum, imperfectly understood but which may be conceptualized (itself a complex idea!) as a network or networks; that is, a biologic system with a structure accepting and producing energy.

Memory and developed idea cannot be easily separated; both are internal representations. As discussed in chapter 4, networks subserving memories of a highly traumatic origin are uniquely encoded and may later exert epileptogenic power or, at least, gain enlargement and dominance. Such memories may become components of more complex ideas and these ideas may gain dominance; or ideas may become dominant, without an obvious connection to an overly arousing memory, but because, for other reasons, they are affectively laden.

REFLEX EPILEPSY

The fact that an idea has a neural locus is further substantiated by reflex epilepsy phenomena. In the reflex epilepsies, a given stimulus, usually external, evokes neuronal excessive discharge of sufficient power that an overt seizure results. The external stimulus then becomes internal, it is mirrored in the brain; it is now internalized in networks. This internal representation, occupying some type of cerebral space, may then also have the capacity to evoke the seizure or at least an EEG response.

In a patient with a left parietal angioma (Goldie and Green, 1959), rubbing the right side of the face produced left parietal spiking on the EEG and generalized seizures beginning focally in right face and upper extremity. When the patient mentally anticipated rubbing his face, the left parietal EEG abnormality appeared as it did when he was asked to imagine rubbing his face.

A patient of Bencze, Troupin, and Prockop (1988) had a vivid memory of an automobile ride when 3 years old; while riding with her parents, the car struck and killed a deer. Later, merely thinking or talking about driving an automobile evoked absence seizures. When she talked about driving, generalized spike and wave activity appeared on the EEG.

These cases are cited to show that networks subserving an idea have a locus. The locus unaided can generate neuronal excessive discharge sufficient to gain the epileptic threshold. Such a locus demonstrates the mirroring or internalizing capacity of the brain. Ideas have a locus and a physiology (Epstein, 1990, 1994). Certain conditions affecting the locus may strengthen the idea so that the idea achieves a powerful position becoming involuntary, repetitive, and of unvarying content. This type of idea may be called an imperative idea (Tuke, 1894).

FETISHISM

There are certain external objects which have the power to evoke intense sexual excitement in humans, particularly males, and their appearance may lead to spontaneous ejaculation: these are fetish objects. The external object becomes mirrored in neuronal networks of the brain. This internal representation appears involuntarily in the mind, a preoccupation often dominating waking consciousness. While it is a source of pleasure, nevertheless such an unbidden image has painful aspects. The involuntary imperative nature of the fetish object and idea suggests they are products of a dominant neuronal circuitry. What factors establish such circuitry?

AROUSING EARLY EVENT

An arousing childhood event, involving the future fetish object, often occurs. The encoding of this event is related, by virtue of its arousal qualities, to the neuronal excessive discharge encountered with the overly vivid catastrophic life events discussed in chapter 4.

A 39-year-old man with boot and raincoat fetishism (Epstein, 1969) dated the onset of his fetishism to early boyhood when he observed, with excitement, his grandfather in boots. He also experienced arousal when handling his grandfather's boots and putting them on. The power of this memory is illustrated by its virtually unaltered appearance in a dream of adulthood. This is in keeping with the discussion in chapter 8 of the appearance of childhood memories in adult dreams, although this memory was more vivid and detailed than most.

I was in this washroom, in the same building in which I played with my grandfather's boots, a very small utility room. I was in the room where my grandfather kept his boots. A picture window on the outside. I was watching. My mother was on the outside. She was hanging clothes on the fence. A big picture window. I could watch her. I proceeded to slip on the boots. At that time I had a wet dream and woke up [p. 81].

As further examples, a woman's hair fetishist recalls the cutting of his hair by his mother at age 3 or 4 and his "excitement in picking up the shorn curls and putting them in a box" (Epstein, 1969). A safety pin fetishist (Mitchell, Falconer, and Hill, 1954) had memories of collecting and playing with "bright, shining safety pins" in early childhood.

QUALITIES OF THE FETISH OBJECT

Certain characteristics of an object seem necessary before it assumes fetish power: the glistening surface of a boot or raincoat; the shape of a shoe; the bare foot (rather than the hand). These are some common fetish objects and perhaps become so because they entrance the child with their bright appearance or novel shape. They have the capacity to arouse and thus to induce unique encoding. These features of the object (Epstein, 1975) become linked to pleasure, to wishes to manipulate, to take in the object, later to sexual arousal, to an insistent pressure in the mind to search for and possess the object.

DOMINANT TEMPOROLIMBIC NEURONAL NETWORKS

The fetish object seems to capture the mechanism which drives sexual arousal and consummatory behavior. Such a mechanism, necessary for species survival, is likely to be temporolimbic in location. There is a clear association between temporolimbic epilepsy and fetishism (Mitchell, Falconer, and Hill, 1954; Epstein, 1961; Hunter, Logue, and McMenemy, 1963). Temporolimbic networks subserving the fetish idea may gain a state of neuronal excessive discharge, thus the involuntary imperative appearance of the fetish in the mind. Such a network is dominant, may enlarge and recruit, eventually attaining a frank seizure threshold.

This is illustrated in the case of safety-pin fetishism described by Mitchell, Falconer, and Hill (1954). "For as long as he could remember" the patient experienced pleasure when looking at a safety pin. Between the ages of 8 and 11, the pleasure was followed by a "blank period." In his twenties, there were episodes in which he was observed to be "glassy-eyed" after staring at the pin; he would make a humming noise and sucking lip movements followed by a brief period of immobility. By age 31, the immobility was followed by automatisms and confusion. The increase in temporolimbic epileptic phenomenology reflects enlargement (recruitment) of a dominant neuronal network; enlargement from the original kernel, the excitement at looking at the safety pin, the original kernel of the network, already the site of neuronal excessive discharge, underlying the fetish representation (Epstein, 1973a). In this patient, seizures only occurred when the safety pin served as a direct stimulus or as a mental image. The evoking of seizures by the safety pin itself or its internalized image-idea is a reflex epilepsy and again testifies to the capacity of the fetish object or idea to produce neuronal excessive discharge sufficient for seizure induction. The fetishism and seizures were abolished by left anterior temporal lobectomy.

GENETIC FACTORS

Still another factor converging to produce the imperative idea of fetishism is the genetic. Phylogenetically, a zoo-dwelling chimpanzee was observed personally (Epstein, 1969) to become sexually aroused—erection, masturbation, and ejaculation—upon seeing and handling a boot (Figure 12.1). Related sexual arousal has been observed in a zoo-dwelling baboon (Figure 12.2). Attachment to a boot, with-

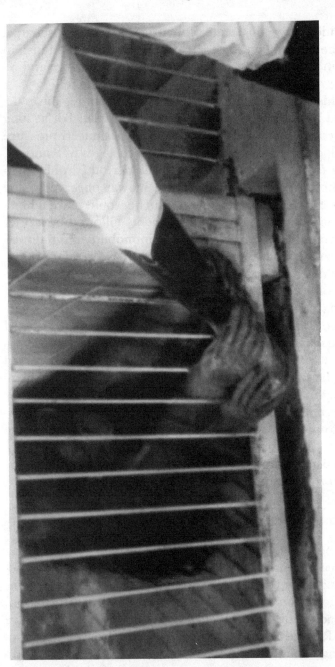

Figure 12.1 Zoo-dwelling chimpanzee displaying interest in and grasping keeper's boot. Erection, self-stimulation, and ejaculation soon follow.

Figure 12.2 Zoo-dwelling baboon displaying interest in keeper's boot. Grasping and oral activity are shown.

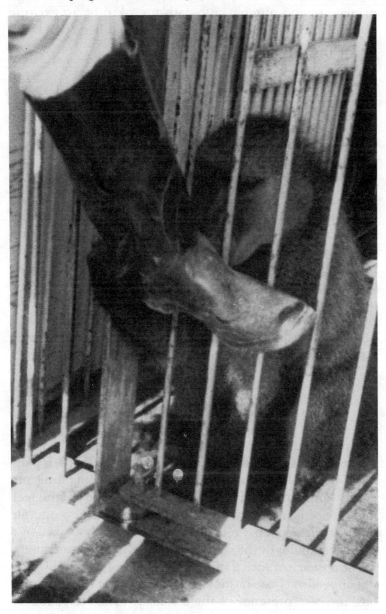

out overt sexual response, has been observed in a gibbon (Epstein, 1987b). Human fetishism may thus represent a high primate temporolimbic automatism evoked by an exciting object. In the genetic context, fetishism has been described in identical twins (Gorman, 1964).

CONDENSATION CAPACITY

In fetishism, we assume a dominant neuronal network, with a capacity for neuronal excessive discharge, subserving the internalized fetish object; its idea. We also assume this network becomes a center to and from which many associative threads are connected; a center of condensation. As a center of condensation, the imperative fetish idea is a symbol. The symbol may represent the mother, father, or another significant figure of early childhood. It may represent a body part: penis, breast, vagina, anus, buttocks. It may have phallic implications (restoration of the castrated genital) (Freud, 1927). With Payne (1939), "every component of the infantile sexual instinct has some connection with the fetish object" (p. 166). The imperative idea of the fetish appears in fantasies and dreams. Its activity is involuntary and insistent.

PHOBIAS

At casual glance, fetishism and phobias appear to be at opposite poles. The fetish object, although its insistence is painful, is primarily endowed with pleasurable feeling tone and evokes approach. Phobias are endowed with the painful feeling tone of fear and evoke avoidance. Phobias also operate on the reflex epilepsy model in that fear is only evoked by a specific stimulus or the stimulus's related category members. In the absence of such a stimulus, the idea of the phobia may not appear in consciousness; it does not have the spontaneous, insistent presence of the fetishistic idea. Nevertheless, the intense fear accompanying the phobic response involuntarily produces the idea of the phobia; then, the idea cannot be inhibited. Phobic ideas, then, qualify as examples of powerful involuntary mentation.

As shown by Lief (1955), a phobia may develop in adult life from the association of an emotionally traumatic event with a certain setting. By associative linkage, the painful emotional event is displaced to the setting so that the setting becomes the phobic object; the setting is feared and avoided. Lief indicates the nature of this encoding tends to set up dominant circuitry.

But there are other etiologic factors in phobias. Childhood animal phobias, as discussed in chapter 11, may stem from innate factors. Such phylogenetic factors, dangers held in common by the human species, form a template, a focus, underlain by dominant neuronal networks, which absorb by associative threads, varied ontogenetic issues, and thus, like the fetish object, become a condensing force, a symbol for these issues.

Phylogenetic Templates

The human fear of heights and of falling produces avoidance, which has survival value since a high perpendicular poses a threat to a large ambulatory organism. This fear is related to changes in visuospatial cues when looking down from a sheer height. Through its strength as an idea and then as a symbol, the fear of falling, as in a dream, may become linked semantically to a "fall" in self-esteem or identity as may accompany a loss of work status (Epstein, 1992).

Similarly, claustrophobia may have phylogenetic roots in the survival threat of inability to leave a small closed space. Having been established either phylogenetically or by a traumatic ontogenetic event, the idea, by semantic linkage, may carry the meaning of a restriction on personal growth.

Agoraphobia may spring phylogenetically from the threat to survival posed by being alone in a large open space without possibility of concealment. Ontogenetically, this may symbolically, by semantic linkage, represent loss of support, of separation, as in fear of loss of a parent.

The same reasoning may be applied to other common phobias such as the fear of darkness, the fear of animals, and the fear of encountering or performing before newly met humans. In the latter case (social phobia), the fear, in a phylogenetic sense, may represent the danger of entering new tribal territories or the fear of humiliation in a dominance–submission context. This innate fear may then symbolically express a sense of guilt, a fancied exposure over some indiscretion.

The Phobic Object

Just as there are fetish objects, so there are phobic (feared) objects. A 38-year-old woman (personal unpublished case) feared needles and straight pins, and particularly feared swallowing a pin inadvertently. She realized this was "foolish," but the fear could not be diminished. She feared friends getting too near her refrigerator lest pins get into the food. Other objects in the "sharp object" category: nails, tacks, and glass were also feared. The pin phobia was exacerbated shortly after the birth of her only child; she feared the infant would swallow a pin. She continued to seek frequent X rays of her daughter for fear pins had been swallowed. Prior to her child's birth, the patient would embroider frequently, using a needle.

This phobia in regard to sharp objects verges on obsessional phenomena in that the objects have aggressive potential, for example, toward her daughter. At the same time, closely identified with the daughter, the patient wishes to protect her daughter, the self, from the feared injurious effects. Although the pin or needle evokes fear, the patient was able to derive pleasure from the use of the needle while embroidering. In some individuals, a given object may have the capacity to evoke both pain (avoidance) and pleasure (approach): This is an ambivalence. Usually, however, avoidance or approach will be the stronger.

The patient feared a straight pin but not a safety pin. The safety pin appears more benign, its sharp component "sheltered," enclosed; it is "safe." A straight pin's sharpness is exposed, apparent. Its potential for harm is clear. The shiny and cunningly designed nature of the safety pin, the sharp point encased, may evoke pleasurable arousal, and indeed as noted, may become a fetish object. In their associative connections, the straight pin may be linked to the phallus; the safety pin to the phallus inserted and contained; safe conjunction.

The references to the safety pin and straight pin in these pages are of interest. In chapter 2, a safety pin was presented for naming to an aphasic patient. The safety pin did not evoke an affective response but, perhaps because of its complexity in form, was not initially comprehended and named correctly. The safety pin became adhesively associated to an object held within the same category, a paper clip. The safety pin became numinous, in the case of Mitchell et al. (1954) and evoked arousal; pleasure because of the setting in which it was encoded and because of the nature of the encoding cerebral tissue. In the patient with needle and straight pin phobia, the safety pin evoked neither pleasurable excitement nor fear.

A safety pin does not ordinarily appear numinous or evoke a strong affective response. This is unlike certain objects, usually animate, which present an uncanny appearance, are not easily comprehended and therefore serve as a symbol, a vehicle for the expression of ideas ordinarily repressed since they lie in deep levels of the unconscious. The human being may be mesmerized by such objects; held in conflict between fleeing (avoidance) and approach (a need to maintain arousal rather than pure pleasure). This arousing intermediate state, this ambivalence between flight and approach may be called fascination. The fascinated individual is drawn to an uncanny, usually novel, potentially dangerous object or creature, the attention compellingly fixed.

A 22-year-old man (Sperling, 1964) preoccupied with snakes, in earlier years kept snakes in cages in his house. Despite his interest and care of snakes, he had frequent disturbing dreams almost entirely of snakes in which he was endangered; for example, bitten. The dreams had powerful, somewhat phobic qualities. He was also sexually stimulated by snakes; the snake, therefore, also had fetish qualities. Like all fetish objects with their dominance, many associative threads were condensed in the snake image and idea. The snake was clearly linked to the penis, also to the vagina and mouth. As may happen with a fetish object, the patient lost self-boundaries, merging with the object, "feeling that he was a snake himself."

Like little Hans' horse and this patient's snake, other creatures evoke fear and become symbolic, "imperative" images in the mind, condensing many threads, associatively linked to archaic material. Little (1967), in his cases of spider phobia, describes a phobic individual's fears of being devoured by the spider, associatively linked to the fear his mother would also do so. Another individual felt he would be sucked in by a spider, a notion associatively linked to his wife. In these two instances, the spider image-idea was associated with the catastrophic early childhood fear of oral incorporation.

The material on the imperative ideas of fetishism and phobias may be summarized as follows:

1. Both fetishistic and phobic ideas bear resemblance to reflex epilepsy phenomena; and, in the case of fetishism, seem a species of temporolimbic neuronal excessive discharge.
2. Factors leading to the establishment of fetish objects are explored.
3. The fetishistic idea has more spontaneous intensity than the phobic. Both are subserved by dominant networks.

4. These dominant networks, particularly in the case of fetishism, have the capacity to recruit; also to exert attraction on other networks.
5. The numerous associative linkages so captured endow fetishistic, and to a lesser extent, phobic mental structures with multiple meaning.

13

Dominant Networks:

The Imperative Ideas of

Obsessive–Compulsive Disorder

The needle and pin phobia described in the previous chapter verges on classical obsessional ideas because of the fear another might be harmed by these objects. In a pure phobia, the individual is concerned almost wholly by fear of self-damage. Concern for hurting another introduces the element of guilt and an element of a "wish to harm," although this wish is not consciously acknowledged. In all instances of obsessive–compulsive disorder, the individual is aware of the irrational nature of the obsessional idea but is unable to banish it from consciousness. Among obsessional ideas, there are several types.

THE FEAR OF
HARMING OTHERS

This is a typical feature of obsessive–compulsive disorder.

1. A 30-year-old man (personal unpublished case) was beset by the fear he would harm or kill others by spreading germs or by other means. This idea was intense, painful, repetitive, filling his mind throughout the day. Some of his involuntary ideas:

Spreading germs by touching another.

Broken glass on a desktop would lead to glass particles on his hand which, by touching, would kill someone.

Opening a door would injure the person immediately behind him.

Paying a person with money he touched would harm the person.

Throwing a piece of paper away would infect the person who would next handle it.

Releasing the ball while bowling would kill a child.

While driving across a bridge, his car might have shoved someone off the bridge.

Becoming contaminated by insecticide in his house and then by touching, killing someone.

Ashes flicked on his pants in a movie house would burn another moviegoer.

Causing a soda bottle to break by touching it, injuring the little girl who was carrying it.

He would be impelled to touch the abdomen of a pregnant woman thus killing the baby in utero.

He washed his hands frequently during the day to remove germs and insecticide.

This symptomatology is typical of obsessive–compulsive disorder but differs from most in that three years before its more florid onset, the patient actually killed a man, a pedestrian who could not be seen, while driving his car. After learning of the death, the patient could not "face" anyone and spent four months almost entirely in bed. There was no clear history of familial obsessive–compulsive disorder although the patient's mother had an inordinate fear of developing cancer.

As noted, this case is unlike the bulk of those with obsessive–compulsive disorder in that an actual catastrophic event occurred. This event produced overwhelming guilty fear. The patient's involuntary ideas are powered by intense guilty fear. Each obsessional fragment is an item in the semantic category of "killing or harming someone." The strength of the guilty fear, after scanning each event, assigns the same meaning to the event; puts each item into the same semantic category.

The emotion of guilty fear is, with pure fear or anxiety itself, the most painful of human emotions. It is associated with activity of the conscience which assigns wrongdoing to an action and anticipates the inevitability of punishment. The individual cringes before punitive conscience. What else can the punishment be but complete abandonment by mother, father, or group? Abandonment is a death feared more than actual death. There is no hope. The surroundings are drained of all color. Relief can only be obtained and this, only in the milder instances, by expiation. (The hedonic state of guilt, as it frequently occurs in dreams is illustrated by dream 3 of chapter 9.)

The power of conscience in the human mind has evolutionary adaptive value. The human is a gregarious organism and must learn restrictions, inhibition, in order to maintain familial and group integrity. Conscience provides the necessary inhibition. The mechanism of conscience requires the capacity to judge the consequences of an act; the engine of conscience is guilty fear. Conscience is a latecomer on the evolutionary road and requires neocortical tissue, probably in the frontal cortex. Frontal lobe development is a uniquely human feature of brain architecture. The influence of the frontal lobes in severe obsessional phenomena was demonstrated, in earlier times, by the amelioration of the forced thoughts and compulsions, by lesioning frontal pathways (Shobe and Gildea, 1968), removing the power of circuitry underlying conscience/guilty fear.

A characteristic of guilty fear, in any human, is that it cannot be easily dispelled and that the idea associated with the guilt is obdurate; neither can be easily dispelled unless expiation is possible. Expiation consists of the confession of the guilt to a parental figure; the parental figure accepts the confession and absolves the guilt. The guilt then, in the normative case, is dissolved as though the dominant network established is temporary and reversible. In our patient, the intensity of the guilt lay beyond the pale of expiation.

Freud (1909b) showed that the obsessional idea is often a compromise formation, a fusion of conflicting emotions. In our case, the thought of hurting or killing contains, beneath the evident guilty fear, the element of aggression, the wish to kill. This wish is repressed, is in the unconscious domain, but is another engine for the power of the obsessional idea. The aggressive wish alerts, through association, conscience and guilty fear, thus perpetuating the obsessional idea. In the normative individual, the homeostatic-tending forces of the mind ("ego") would be able to dismiss the idea, by suppression or repression, by their capacity to contain the two opposing forces, aggression and guilt, preventing the independent opposing activity of aggression-guilt, thus eliminating the intensity of the obsessional idea.

In our patient, a dominant network must be involved to account for the intensity and persistence of the obsessional idea; but the nature of the dominant network seems different from those described in earlier chapters. We are not dealing simply with fear, a pure brute survival threat, or with the encoding of such a threat. Instead, we are dealing with a more complex state, guilt as well as fear, and with the presence of aggressive forces in the unconscious domain. The imperative idea in obsessive–compulsive disorder may not simply be the product of an excessively discharging network but rather of "release" of network activity freed from normal inhibition.

Conscience/guilty fear mechanisms seem innate (have genetically determined networks) in humans, not to say they are not learned, but even then, the potential for such learning is innate. If there is some imbalance in basal ganglia-thalamo-fronto-cortical circuits (Baxter, Phelps, Mazziotta, Guze, Schwartz, and Selin, 1987), this might accentuate the power of conscience/guilty fear mechanisms either by amplifying them or by weakening control mechanisms. When a control mechanism is weakened, the released force (in Jacksonian doctrine) emerges with crude strength (Jackson, 1882). Dominant networks in this type of obsessive–compulsive disorder may then reflect a release phenomenon.

THE FEAR OF PUNISHMENT

2. A 42-year-old man (personal unpublished case) was "tortured" by the thought that he would be sent to jail. This thought was accompanied by intense fear disrupting waking consciousness. Varied stimuli evoked this guilty fear, this certainty of guilt, despite the patient's recognition his reaction was "foolish":

> He feared he would sexually attack a young girl seen on the street, leading to his being jailed.

> He would punch an old lady seen on the street and this would lead to his being jailed.

> He feared he would shout out an obscenity.

> He feared he would hit a pregnant woman and be sent to jail.

> Seeing the word *incorporated* led to the thought of a company he worked for, in turn leading to concern over an error he might have made there, leading to the fear he would be put in jail.

> Thinking of a "dead boy on the battlefield" led to the thought, "that could be my son," leading to "you think that because you want to kill your son."

He would ring a fire alarm and go to jail.

He feared that he had hit someone with his car and would go to jail.

The terminus of virtually all these painful involuntary thoughts is punishment by jailing. It is as though there is a dominant network subserving this idea, and that the network attracts any likely stimulus, incorporating it into the semantic category of "going to jail." The power maintaining this dominant network is guilty fear.

In addition, the patient has a rapidity and fluidity of association indicating a dysinhibition over associative regulation (an unusual ease of connectivity). Possibly also contributing to the phenomenology is a hypermnesia, the patient recalling details of events (including telephone numbers) of many years past. Such a hypermnesia may also be related to the lack of inhibition over associations; to heightened cerebral cortical "reflex" activity.

This case is similar to case 1 although there is less emphasis on the danger of touching and contaminating. As in case 1, aggressive impulses are present but are not truly recognized, remaining primarily in the unconscious domain. Unlike case 1, there is no clear precipitant to the obsessional disorder. Family history revealed the patient's mother expressed frequent guilt and feared leaving the house.

TABOO AND SEMANTIC LINKAGES

Patient 2 feared he might shout out an obscenity (coprolalia). Many obsessional patients fear this, particularly when in church or other hallowed places. It is a taboo to defile a holy place with an obscenity. The firmer and the more powerful the prohibition, the stronger the impulse to violate the prohibition. The same situation holds in cases 1 and 2 where there was an impulse to touch or hit a pregnant woman. This also violates a powerful prohibition.

Taboos are universal but are omnipresent in less developed societies (Frazer, 1922) and serve to maintain social structures, particularly those whose overthrow would be catastrophic. Indeed Freud (1913) noted the similarity, if not identity, of taboo and obsessional disorder; for example, taboos against touching.

In a taboo situation, the individual is aware of the prohibition, the catastrophic consequences of violating the prohibition, and is simultaneously aware of the action which would violate the taboo. The arousal produced by the taboo intensifies the wish to action. The prohibition and the wish to commit tabooed action are coupled. They are associatively linked. Just as in the aphasia described in chapter 2 where linkages were formed on a phonemic and crude semantic basis, so, as we ascend to the complexity of symbolic ideation, the basic mental process of connectivity remains operative; complex ideational categories are associatively linked. This accounts for the binding of prohibition and action, particularly in obsessional patients where inhibition over this binding is impaired; impaired homeostasis, impaired function of higher centers (the "ego").

COPROLALIA

As noted, the impulse to utter an obscenity reflects the taboo mechanism. Obscenities are deep aggressions, substitutes or equivalents of physical aggressions, and are generally reserved for situations in which the expression of aggression is homeostatic (tension-reducing). Coprolalia is found in obsessive–compulsive disorder and is clinically and genetically related to Tourette's. The coprolalic impulse is powerful because the word striving for utterance is coded with deep emotion—precisely the type of structure against which a powerful control mechanism (prohibition) must be erected. These two strong adversaries produce a marked internal struggle, particularly in states of dysinhibition as in obsessive–compulsive disorder and Tourette's.

THE NEED FOR CLOSURE OF CATEGORICAL NETWORKS

This is a typical feature of obsessive–compulsive disorder. A word or idea or action must be realized to bring relief to an ever-mounting sense of inner tension. Three cases are examples:

3. A 36-year-old woman (personal unpublished case) with complex partial seizures and accompanying obsessive–compulsive disorder, has an agonizing need to think:

> When you mention lists, I thought of pencil and paper and I thought—these are supplies.

> The children were talking about candy. "I had to understand candy." Then "I know I have candy at home. I have to use money to buy candy. I have money here and money at home."

> Discussing a camping trip, the patient thought of "tent" then "a tent is like a house. My brother has a trailer. It's like a house, it's like a car."

> When thinking of a clock, she must think, "Clock in house. Clock is part of house. They tell time. Sometimes I don't understand time. Time inside you. I can't understand 'clock.'"

> When thinking of food, she must think "Food. Home. Food is part of home."

> The patient reports confusion unless she can adequately classify. When thinking of bike, she needs to think, "that's a toy," she then feels "better." Similarly upon thinking of the word *recipe*, "that's food."

"I have to understand what the bed is. I think, 'This is part of house.'" The patient then feels satisfied.

It's hard to understand "taking medicine." The patient must think "It's me, I'm taking it, I'm taking it with water. Water is something you understand."

The patient has counting rituals which help her to "understand." Similarly, there is a compulsion to make lists. Failure to go through these and the cognitive procedures mentioned is "terrifying." A paternal aunt is "afraid" of dirt, germs, and pesticides.

4. A 31-year-old man (personal unpublished case) has several obsessions and compulsions, primarily "I have to know." This is achieved by repeated questioning of people and further observations. As an example, "If I see someone with a shirt, I must know, is it a button-down?" He then must "check" to see if it is a button-down. If he sees a food display at the supermarket, "I have to go back to know what it (the name and price) was." If he cannot know, "it turns over and over in my mind and I can't sleep." Onset of this imperative need was at age 25 without clear precipitating cause.

Both the patient and his younger brother have an identical compulsion: "to pick up trash"; for example, paper in the street.

5. A 48-year-old woman (Epstein, 1994) with obsessional thoughts and compulsions since late childhood, experiences anxiety when she meets someone with a "bad" proper name. Anxiety mounts until one with a "good" name is found; anxiety then completely subsides. She also has the capacity to remember past events in great detail (a hypermnesia).

In these three cases, there is an imperative need to think of related associated items, to construct categories for these items, to gain certainty. It is as though there is a cerebral cortical network subserving associated items within a category—that this network is open-ended and needs to attract associated items to fill positions in the network. The network needs additional associated items in order to enlarge, perhaps to permit closure of the network, to seal the open positions. Enlargement and closure may represent a characteristic physiological activity of neuronal networks (Epstein, 1994).

In case 3, there is an imperative need to place items within a category. There is also a need to generate additional items in the same category similar to the obligatory associations of dreaming described in chapter 8. Further, there is an imperative need to "understand" an object, as though the usual initial exposure is not sufficient to "embed" the object or concept. The network is not sufficiently receptive or stable to permit "embedding"; this can only be achieved by gaining more associations or establishing their position in a category.

In case 4 there is a need to know, to be certain. Initial exposure does not embed. Questioning or further observation is essential to embed, perhaps to close a network.

In case 5, the network is closed by finding a "good" or pleasurable item to replace a "bad" or painful one. This replacement, one conjectures, closes a network. Both "good" and "bad" items are associatively linked by contrast within the same category, the category of proper names.

In these three cases, there again appears to be a dysregulation, a lack of modulation of cerebral cortical neuronal network physiology, of networks subserving the categorical organization of associated items. Whether or not there is a primary excitability of networks or whether there is a release of networks from their usual inhibitory mechanisms is not clear. Increased cerebral cortical activity as measured by glucose metabolic rates has been demonstrated by Baxter et al. (1987), in obsessive–compulsive disorder. Rates were significantly increased in the orbital region of the left frontal lobe and in the caudate nuclei.

The notion that the associative dyscontrol, the "reflex" imperative ideation of obsessive–compulsive disorder is a product of abnormal cortical excitation or of release is further strengthened by the occurrence of seemingly similar forced ideation during seizural neuronal excessive discharge.

6. A 30-year-old woman's (personal unpublished case) generalized seizures began with forced ideation. "I may look at a thing, for example, the ashtray, and have crazy thoughts about it. For example, does the ashtray walk?" These thoughts cannot be dispelled.

7. A 21-year-old man's (personal unpublished case) seizures began with unbidden thoughts. "I might look at the wastebasket and look and look at it and wonder how far over the side of the basket the paper (inner wrapping) is. I might also wonder why there is paper in the basket in the first place."

The material on the imperative ideas of obsessive–compulsive disorder may be summarized as follows:

1. There are varied forms of obsessive–compulsive disorder. In some, involuntary obsessional thoughts are powered by guilty fear, in turn, powered by aggressive forces. Aggression, a deeply coded instinctual drive, is the chief forbidden impulse encountered.
2. Conscience/guilty fear and aggressive drive are associatively linked, bound together. This linkage is evident in obsessive–compulsive disorder and in taboo phenomena.
3. Another form of obsessive–compulsive disorder reflects a need for closure and/or expansion of categorical networks.
4. The imperative nature of association formation in obsessive–compulsive disorder is a reflection of increased cerebral cortical network activity. Such activity, outside awareness and volition, is due to increased endogenous excitation of cortical cells or their release from usual control mechanisms.

14

Origins and Transmission of Imperative Ideas

If, as we assume, imperative ideas are subserved by neural structures called networks, we ask how these networks come to exist in an individual. This has been partially answered in previous chapters, in terms of the unique encoding of a catastrophic event creating neuronal excessive discharge in a network with resultant dominance. One cause therefore is ontogenetic trauma. What role a predisposed nervous system plays (the "constitutional" factor) introduces another element. One such predisposition is an impairment in control mechanisms releasing lower centers, permitting stereotyped, involuntary, emotionally crude ideation. Control mechanisms may also be impaired in states of lowered mood or heightened anxiety.

In childhood particularly an event is more likely to be significantly arousing, and acting on brain tissue of some immaturity, memory of the event achieves vividness and may develop into an imperative idea. This is a factor in the origin of imperative phobic and fetishistic ideas. The appearance of childhood memories in dreams (chapter 8) also testifies to their power.

The degree of arousal accompanying the encoding of an event, whether in childhood or adulthood, depends upon the event's linkage to the intense emotions generated at the instinctual level (the phylogenetic impress): the instincts, for example, associated with erotic pleasure (as in the encoding of the fetish object); with survival fear (as in the encoding of the phobic object); and with social behavior (as in the conscience–aggression taboo complex). An attempt will now be made, through consideration of genetic factors, to deepen the view of how an individual comes to be a bearer of imperative ideas, a bearer of dominant networks.

TRANSMISSION BY GENETIC FACTORS

Epilepsy is a manifestation of neuronal excessive discharge. In temporolimbic epilepsy, the seizure content may contain complex ideational or perceptual material, appearing involuntarily. Barslund and Danielson (1963) described such seizure content in monozygotic twins. Even though the literature on larger samples of temporolimbic epileptics, in terms of genetic factors, is far from clear, the study of smaller samples, individual and familial, while criticized by keen methodologists as "anecdotal," nevertheless offers a time-honored entry into the nature of clinical phenomenology. The appearance of similar or identical phenomena in each of monozygotic twins is considered evidence of a genetic mechanism.

Barsland and Danielson studied three pairs of monozygotic twins. In the first, both felt a sensation of "strangeness" in association with their seizures. In the second, both experienced a sensation of déjà vu, apparently postictal. In the third, the twins themselves did not display identical seizure phenomena, but one and the daughter of the other monozygotic twin had virtually identical seizural perceptual–affective phenomena. These complex phenomena occurred recurrently as a seizure component.

The twin experienced herself "in a company of five to ten adults, talking with them, seeing them, but being unable to describe them afterwards. Something was discussed which upset her, but afterwards she was unable to remember what it was."

The daughter of the other twin experienced "many people fighting with one another, screaming and shouting in a street scene." This experience was frightening.

Although these dysphoric seizural visual experiences occurred in the daughter rather than the monozygotic mother, a genetic tie is assumed. The similarities of the seizural experience, a group of people in some type of discord, painful in nature, is striking. The imagery is dreamlike as may be the case in certain temporolimbic seizures. Occurring as a seizure component, the imagery is a product of neuronal excessive discharge. As a recurrent seizure component, it is likely that a dominant network has been established in two genetically related individuals. The network subserves a complex imaginal–ideational fragment.

As noted previously, recurrent dysphoric dreams, usually typical, seem to share a similar neuronal substratum with temporolimbic seizures. Familial dream studies, however, are rare (Epstein and Collie, 1976).

A 24-year-old woman always had recurrent "bad dreams" of typical theme: flying, the object endangered (car accidents). When awakened from REM periods, other typical themes were unearthed: her husband was endangered, she feared her daughter would drown, she helped set a fire. Her 20-year-old sister described recurrent dreams of typical theme: finding her mother dead, falling. The third sister, age 35, reported recurrent dysphoric dreams with typical themes: death of significant others, inability to control a car.

The father of the three sisters, now deceased, had disturbing dreams, apparently recurrent: chasing or being chased, being attacked. He shouted in his sleep. His grandmother also talked and screamed in her sleep.

Here, there is an intergenerational dream disturbance, a failure of modulation, affecting, at least, a father and three daughters. The dreams are recurrent and typical. One suspects a genetic transmission of dominant networks. Content is not precisely identical except in the car dreams of two of the sisters.

In addition to dominant network activity in temporo-limbic seizures and certain dream types, such activity may underlie imperative waking ideation. Here too, the bearers of such ideation may be recipients of genetic transmission.

Woodruff and Pitts (1964) described monozygotic twins with an identical need to precisely align scatter rugs. Both had unwanted forced thoughts concerning morality or good-ness. Their father seemed similarly affected.

Monozygotic twins reported by Marks, Crowe, Drewe, Young, and Dewhurst (1969), had identical obsessional thoughts: fear of contamination by dogs.

Gorman (1964) described rubber fetishism in monozy-gotic twins, developing independently without knowledge of the other's fetishism. Each developed rubber fetishism at the same period of childhood (ages 5–6) following a pleasurable episode of arousal: the one with a rubber cot sheet, the other with a rubber cape. Some type of intergenerational transmis-sion of fetishistic behavior is suggested by the fact the twins' father "on occasion wore a lady's fox fur collar."

Individual family studies also suggest the likelihood of genetic transmission. Sanders (1973) reported father and son with Tourette's syndrome; both had coprolalia. The father uttered obscenities but struggled against them "by grinding his teeth, barking or yelling." The son had intrusions of ob-scene words into consciousness (the obsessional idea) but, almost identically, suppressed actual utterances by "barking, grunting or coughing." Since the coprolalic utterance and the struggle for control are very private matters with inde-pendent onset, a genetic factor is likely in these two virtu-ally identical cases.

Besides fetishism, the sexual deviations include trans-vestism, exhibitionism, pedophilia, and extreme sadomaso-chism; all are "imperative," stereotyped, occasionally "unwanted," and, historically, usually derived from an initial arousing experience with subsequent fixation. The arousing experience, a unique encoding on a predisposed brain, finds later expression as a dominant network.

Buhrich (1977) described father and son who both cross-dressed and had wishes to become women. This activity and ideation appeared independently without evidence of imitation. Krueger (1978) reported fetishistic–transvestitic behavior in a father and four sons. Although the author considered the etiology identificatory, a genetic factor is likely. Comings and Comings (1982) reported exhibitionism, apparently developing independently, in father and son. Another familial instance of exhibitionism was described by Shapiro (1980).

Suicide may present as an imperative idea and is often familial. Zaw (1981) described male identical twins who committed suicide; their father made a serious suicide attempt; both paternal and maternal grandfathers committed suicide.

As one considers larger samples, confirmation of familial incidence is gained by such large familial studies as those of Gaffney, Lurie, and Berlin (1984) on pedophilia; Lewis (1935) on obsessive–compulsive disorder; Roy (1983) on suicide; Solyom, Beck, Solyom, and Hugel (1974) on phobias. These studies indicate intergenerational transmission of imperative ideas, a transmission which may employ a genetic mechanism (Epstein, 1987–1988). Such a mechanism would follow complex but traditional lines. In terms of genetic explanations, we have also, in previous chapters, noted the phylogenetic component, a component closely bound to individual and species survival, arising far back in the historical past, perhaps as far as preprimate organisms.

TRANSMISSION OF ACQUIRED CATASTROPHIC TRAUMA

Is there another genetic pathway, one that can be acquired in an individual's lifetime and then transmitted? The basis for this question is the observation that a catastrophic life event affects offspring of parents who experienced and survived that event. Again, the catastrophic event presumes a unique encoding leading to the creation of a dominant network subserving an imperative idea. Genetic transmission of this type is Lamarckian, a concept unacceptable to current genetic theory. To sustain such a notion, one must first seek a catastrophic event and then search for imperative dreams and/or waking ideas of that event in children born after the event; children of parents who endured and then survived such an event.

Such an event is the Holocaust (Epstein, 1982). The overwhelming impress of the Holocaust experience has been described by Niederland (1968); the "survivor syndrome." A high incidence of psychiatric disorder has been found in the children of survivors. This includes specific images of the Holocaust arising involuntarily.

A daughter of two survivors had, since childhood, "been plagued by nightmares of men chasing her and her family. She still had nightmares about members of her family dying or being killed" (H. Epstein, 1979). Winnick (1968) described a son of survivors who "had nightmares which resembled in content the typical dreams of persecutees." Axelrod, Schnipper, and Rau (1980) studied thirty children of survivors finding "the frequent use of concentration camp imagery occurred in almost every survivor child." Some reported "fantasies and nightmares dealing with sadomasochistic captor–captive roles." Kestenberg (1972) mentioned "a survivor-mother, who complained that both she and her daughter suffered from repeated nightmares." Wardi (1992) described in detail her psychotherapy with children of Holocaust survivors, the transmission of the Holocaust traumas to these children, and the manifestation of these traumas in the children's dreams and mental phenomena. An example from one such dream (Wardi, 1992):

I'm in a concentration camp, in a huge hall that looks like a storage room. The ceiling is very high and near the top there are these tiny windows. Along the walls, lower down, there are bookcases piled with books. We were there, in this room, a few people, all of us very thin, complete skeletons. Everyone was spread out on the floor like a sack, because no one had the strength to move. I am about twelve years old (the age at which Miriam's mother was taken to the camp). All my bones stuck out of my body . . . [pp. 136–137].

This dream with its specific description of the concentration camp hall as well as of the prisoners could conceivably be reproducing a memory of extrapersonal origin.

Although the contents of the unconscious may consist primarily of memories, ideation, and action tendencies acquired during ontogeny, and although uncanny images arising in dreams, when there is loss of modulation, may represent the vividness of early childhood memories, some dream material seems to lie beyond the arena of childhood alone. This vivid material has a phylogenetic impress and has already been noted in typical dreams (chapter 7). Is it also possible that certain dreams, for example, of being mutilated, being tortured, being invaded by animals (chapters 10, 11) represent actual events endured by members of the human species in history, memories acquired and then transmitted as dominant networks to subsequent generations?

To dream of a "brightly colored parrot" (chapter 10) might simply represent an image arising from daily life, that is, an item from the day residue. But the fascinating and uncanny nature of the parrot image may stem from its hold on minds of previous generations—assimilated by them as an arousing and unique encoding, buried, lying deep in the unconscious, appearing again only when there is a significant impairment in modulation.

All students of the unconscious seek comprehension of these phenomena. Freud (1913) conceptualized the Oedipus complex as arising from an actual ancient event: the anguished struggle of father and sons, the killing of the father by a band of sons. Such an event, if at all actual, would require unique encoding and, if transmitted genetically, does so through a Lamarckian mechanism. Jung (1953) conceptualized the collective unconscious as a container of memories, images, and ideas, a container of ancient experiences of the human species.

In chapter 11, three women independently reported dreams of torture and mutilation following thiothixene administration (Solomon, 1983). Such dreams had never been previously experienced by these individuals. What is their origin? Assume the thiothixene molecule influences a dominant network either by further exciting it (neuronal excessive discharge) or by removing an inhibitory force (repression). As a result, images subserved by the network enter dream awareness: a failure of modulation. What is the origin of such a network? In pursuing our notion further, assume an actual event involving torture and mutilation occurring in the historical past to ancestors of these women. Such an event would be catastrophic and therefore encoded uniquely. It becomes dominant and has the capacity to be transmitted through an as yet unknown genetic mechanism to subsequent generations. The dominant network after its transmission demands inhibition (repression) in order to reduce unbearable dysphoria, to maintain mental homeostasis; the repression only able to be overcome by a specific chemical action.

Such a mechanism of Lamarckian nature would explain the accrual of new memories (networks) in human history, their storage in sufficient individuals to become contents of the collective unconscious, storage at the deepest levels of the unconscious.

Again, another dream of uncanny nature: "troupes of women who seem to swarm about his bed and try to choke him" cited in chapter 10 (Daniels, 1934) may then represent an ancestral memory, unearthed by a failure in modulation, a memory encoding an actual event, strange to us, because of the different ways, setting, rituals of bygone days, incidents shrouded in mystery. Such events may be shrouded in mystery but are still subject to the powers of secondary elaboration.

The material on the origins and transmission of imperative ideas may be summarized as follows:

1. Monozygotic twin and familial studies suggest a genetic factor in the origin of dominant networks and their manifestations as imperative ideas and dreams.
2. The possibility of the transmission of acquired catastrophic trauma, of acquired dominant networks, is posed. This concept is speculative and the genetic mechanisms involved uncertain. A related speculation is the possibility of transmission of ancestral memories.

15

Implications for Psychodynamic Science

Rado (1956) called for the creation of a true psychodynamic science, defined as the study of human motivation and control. The data of this science are gained by introspective methods, and represent the cerebral cortex in action. Psychodynamics is a basic science of the organism. The forces of motivation and control rest upon neurochemical, neurophysiological, and genetic pillars. More broadly, psychodynamic science is the study of the workings of the mind. Varied implications can be drawn from previous chapters that enlarge the structure of psychodynamic science particularly as understood by the clinician.

The essential psychodynamic forces are the associative mechanism, the inclusion of memories in the associative mechanism, the influence of affect (elaborations of pleasure-pain) in giving weight to particular items in the associative mechanism, and the hierarchically superior homeostatic function with its attendant capacity to initiate and develop concepts.

ASSOCIATIVE MECHANISMS

In a depth psychotherapeutic clinical setting, if left unencumbered, there is associative flow. Interruption or deviation of

149

the flow may be viewed as an affective leverage, a homeostatic, although miscarried, function. Ideally, the flow is determined by the unconscious; it is a product of involuntary connections. There may, of course, be volitional selection of certain items; the resistance may operate through an unconscious homeostatic mechanism or through volitional avoidance.

Connections may be formed at an elementary semantic or phonemic level but also at a complex semantic (high categorical) level. The connections at the latter level, perhaps less tenacious than those at the more elementary level, are nevertheless sufficiently so to establish habitual modes of thought.

If maladaptive, associative linkages at the complex semantic (high categorical) level may be weakened by verbal exteriorization with affective accompaniment, by encouragement, by appealing to pleasure–reward mechanisms (ego strengthening).

Increasing ego strength may diminish the power of unbidden connectivity. Similarly, the diminution of ego strength, the weakening of forces of control by the dysphoria of guilty fear or anxiety, permits crude connectivity to flourish, as in depression where painful memories or ideas, categorically linked, appear in recurrent stereotyped fashion. Euphoria powers pleasurable memories and associative items (categories); dysphoria, painful memories and associative items (categories).

TRAUMATIC MEMORIES

Recurrent memories of catastrophic events may have their associated painful affects reduced by verbal exteriorization with profound emotional release. The beneficial effect of such abreaction was described by Breuer and Freud (1895) in their studies of hysteria; symptomatology was traced to earlier traumatic events and relieved by bringing the event into awareness, at first through hypnosis and later through the paths of waking association.

Thus, abreaction alone is able to diminish the dominance of a network, perhaps by decreasing its contained neuronal excessive discharge. This concept, although expressed differently, is implied in the theories of Breuer and Freud. Perhaps abreaction also weakens the bonds, the energy, between items joined to each other in categorical networks; perhaps entire networks may be weakened with the discharge of energy.

DREAMING

Increased recognition of associative dysinhibition and associative formation in dreaming enhances appreciation of the dream's cognitive functions. However, since affective influence on associative items is clear, the cognitive–emotional aspects of dreaming remain vital in psychodynamic understanding and psychotherapeutic use. The frequent appearance of "typical" imagery also enhances appreciation of the transpersonal factors in dreaming but does not diminish the use of this manifest content by the dreamer to express significant strivings, and therefore justifies the necessity to trace out the varied associative threads offered. Recurrent typical themes reflect dominant circuitry produced not only by phylogenetic influences but also, in some cases, by an earlier ontogenetic catastrophic event, therefore requiring a search for such an event.

TEMPLATES

Typical dream imagery is a focus for many associative threads, for example in the "something happening to the teeth" dream, many meanings are ascribed to this imagery. Such imagery may be considered a template in that it serves as a mold or pattern, a structure composed of many threads, an overarching structure with subordinate components. The mind seems organized into templates, which serve as foci of condensation. A template, an associative structure, which attracts many networks is a dominant structure. The concept of templates, dominant networks subject to analysis, is illustrated not only by typical dream imagery but also by the internalizations of fetish and phobic objects, and by the ideation of obsessive–compulsive disorder.

INTERNALIZATION

The brain has the capacity to mirror an external object or event, to internalize them. The internal locus may have the same physiological energy as the external, a phenomenon illustrated by reflex epilepsy. This internalizing capacity is of importance for it underlies mechanisms of identification, the "taking in" of another person or even of an idea. Without volition, attributes of another are assimilated. Assimilation may occur at the cruder level of imitation or through a process of unknowing, subtle influence. This incorporation of others, introjects, develops the ego–self system.

    Introjects provide models, templates for growth. Introjects associated with pleasure, with safety, have intrapsychic stabilizing value; they maintain homeostasis. Some introjects may be voluntarily brought into awareness for their stabilizing and anxiety-dispelling value. Internalizations underlie development of personal identity.

GENETIC INFLUENCES

The data clearly indicating familial impress and, likely, phylogenetic influence, enlarge the field of psychodynamic forces. If genetic factors are important, not only for formation of temperament-character but also for that of involuntary mentation, even beyond the psychopathological, there must be some alteration of focus in clinical comprehension and management.

Although the search for significant ontogenetic events, particularly the traumatic, must continue and be explored, mental characteristics and certain symptom complexes have a genetic basis in the neural substratum. Although broadening etiologic understanding, the presence of genetic factors need not deter a vigorous psychotherapeutic approach. Abreactive and related techniques, as well as providing homeostasis-tending object constancy, may affect neuronal networks even genetically formed. Accurate etiologic formulations must be bolstered by a careful family history.

The phylogenetic influence is drawn from the nature of temporolimbic seizure content and from typical dream content. This content indicates a primacy of survival concerns; concerns of meeting external physical challenges or of maintaining life-sustaining object relationships. The key psychodynamic goal is survival. Fear is a potent alerting signal to danger or threat. Dysphoric anxiety dreams appear maladaptive on the surface, but they increase vigilance and protective behavior (Epstein, 1987a).

Survival must be insured before erotic pleasure can be approached. Therefore, libidinal energies are not the prime engines of motivation although they are not inconsiderable since species survival is also nature's concern. Survival permeates all motivation even though the concerns, more manifestly, are ego–self maintenance and enhancement, the securing and development of interpersonal relationships, the anguish of separation.

MODULATION AND INTEGRATION

In the hierarchical structure of the central nervous system and its product, mentation, the highest levels seem involved with modulation (homeostasis) and integration. These are currently designated as "ego" functions, chiefly involuntary and therefore unconscious. Likely, they are mediated by the frontal lobes.

This modulating and integrating force is expressed in the dream as secondary revision with its ideational and imaginal sequencing as well as in some degree of pain–pleasure regulation. It is also expressed in waking awareness by employment of safeguards or defenses and by the capacity to integrate opposing semantic associative structures.

Impairments of modulation and integration permit crude ideas and images to enter dream or waking awareness and give preponderance to underlying crude associative processes as first mentioned in the aphasias, later in dreams and psychopathologies. Among the psychopathologies, for sake of wider application, Hoffman, Oates, Hafner, Hustig and McGlashan (1994) noted recurrent content of semantically associated items in the hallucinated voices of schizophrenic individuals. The voices of one patient, for example, said, on separate occasion, "fat," "hungry," "eat," "garbage," "guts," all associated items in the category of "obesity and eating." In this instance, a category specific network is either released from inhibition or otherwise activated to permit its unfettered expression—as has been described in aphasia and the epilepsies.

TEMPORARY DOMINANT NETWORKS

The concept of dominant networks implies persistence of stereotyped involuntary ideas, but such ideas may also be time limited. An example is bereavement. The shock of death, the loss of a beloved, consumes the mind with grief. Powerful involuntary ideas appear, unrelenting and difficult to dispel. The ideas revolve about the lost individual. Slowly the intensity of the ideas diminishes, with eventual resolution. The intense emotion generated by the loss seems to have established a dominant network which is time limited. There is, then, a capacity for reversibility in certain dominant networks.

Similarly, in endogenous depression where mood-lowering prevents the inhibition of ruminative ideas, ideas held in association by the common element of guilty fear (in the same semantic category), these fade as the depression lifts and mood heightens.

FANTASY COMPARED TO DREAMING

Fantasy and dream are usually dissociated. The content of fantasy often does not penetrate the dream mechanism. The two are functioning at different hierarchical levels.

The influence of the day residue, the involuntary unfolding of associations as a product of dysinhibition, the involuntary workings of secondary revision, distinguish dreaming from fantasy. Fantasy is generally initiated voluntarily; it is an act of the imagination for which one bears responsibility. Therefore, revelation of fantasy to another is likely to produce shame. Because of its involuntary nature, a dream is revealed with less shame.

Fantasy, however, through its own associative mechanisms, may recruit items from the unconscious. Although usually voluntarily shaped, fantasies may become recurrent and stereotyped. Fantasy is a private waking activity which serves an adaptive purpose by permitting the emergence into awareness of instinctual strivings, permitting their expression without action with another, without suffering the punishment of social forces or of those conscience mechanisms primarily responsive to social forces.

THERAPEUTIC CONSIDERATIONS

Since psychodynamic science rests on the genetic and neural pillars underlying the play of mental forces, therapeutic measures have a wide range of application. The concepts of associative dysinhibition and of neuronal excessive discharge indicate that therapeutic leverage should be designed to influence these causes of psychopathology. This has been achieved. The earliest method was dyadic psychotherapeutics; the expression and abreaction by hypnotic and nonhypnotic means designed, in effect, to unload the energy, the "neuronal excessive discharge" engendered by the encoding of traumatic events (Breuer and Freud, 1895). Psychotherapeutic treatment also strengthens homeostatic forces through internalization and ego mastery. Simple hypnotic suggestion serves a similar purpose.

Next, electroconvulsive therapy was employed, particularly in the treatment of major depression, mood lowering with its accompanying ruminative and involuntary ideas, chiefly powered by guilty fear. Although the nature of the therapeutic effect of producing a convulsion, an overwhelming neuronal excessive discharge, is not clear, it is likely that the generalized convulsion disrupts the dominance of certain networks underlying the symptomatology.

Next, pharmacologic discoveries have directly addressed the problem of neuronal excessive discharge through the development of modulators with their anticonvulsant properties and have also addressed problems of associative dyscontrol, dysharmonies within and between categorical networks, through molecular actions affecting transmission at neuronal synapses and adhesion at their receptors. The effectiveness of such compounds has been demonstrated in the treatment of such psychopathologies as obsessive–compulsive disorder in which effects on synaptic transmission have been demonstrated. Involuntary mentation is clearly influenced by psychopharmacologic agents and even more specific influences are anticipated in the future.

Implications of the study of dreaming and involuntary mentation for psychodynamic science may be summarized as follows:

1. Associative and homeostatic mechanisms are further scrutinized, and the implications of genetic influences discussed.
2. Concepts of templates, temporary dominant networks and of a neural basis for mental internalization are introduced.
3. A brief comparison between dream and fantasy is made.
4. General therapeutic considerations in the treatment of imperative ideas are presented.

References

Alkon, D. L. (1975), Neural correlates of associative training in Hermissenda. *J. Gen. Physiol.*, 65:46–56.

Aring, C. D. (1968), Intimations of mortality: An appreciation of death and dying. *Ann. Intern. Med.*, 69:137–152.

Aserinsky, E., & Kleitman, N. (1955), Two types of ocular motility occurring in sleep. *J. Appl. Physiol.*, 8:1–10.

Axelrod, S., Schnipper, O. L., & Rau, J. H. (1980), Hospitalized offspring of Holocaust survivors. *Bull. Menninger Clin.*, 44:1–14.

Barslund, I., & Danielsen, J. (1963), Temporal epilepsy in monozygotic twins. *Epilepsia*, 4:138–150.

Bartemeier, L. H. (1950), Illness following dreams. *Internat. J. Psycho-Anal.*, 31:8–11.

Basso, A., Capitani, E., & Laiacona, M. (1988), Progressive language impairment without dementia: A case with isolated category specific semantic defect. *J. Neur. Neurosurg. Psychiatry*, 51:1201–1207.

Baxter Jr., L. R., Phelps, M. E., Mazziotta, J. C., Guze, B. H., Schwartz, J. M., & Selin, C. E. (1987), Local cerebral glucose metabolic rates in obsessive–compulsive disorder. *Arch. Gen. Psychiatry*, 44:211–225.

Bell, W. L., Horner, J., Logue, P., & Radtke, R. A. (1990), Neologistic speech automatisms during complex partial seizures. *Neurology*, 40:49–52.

Benzce, K. S., Troupin, A., & Prockop, L. D. (1988), Reflex absence epilepsy. *Epilepsia*, 29:48–51.

Bliss, T. V. P., & Lomo, T. (1973), Long-lasting potentiation of synaptic transmission in the dentate area of the anaesthetized rabbit following stimulation of the perforant path. *J. Physiology*, 232:331–356.

Breuer, J., & Freud, S. (1895), Studies on Hysteria. *Standard Edition*, 2. London: Hogarth Press, 1955.

Brock, S., & Wiesel, B. (1941), The narcoleptic-cataplectic syndrome—an excessive and dissociated reaction of the sleep mechanism—and its accompanying mental states. *J. Nerv. Ment. Dis.*, 94:700–712.

Buhrich, N. (1977), A case of familial heterosexual transvestism. *Acta Psychiat. Scand.*, 55:199–201.

Clark, L. P. (1915), The nature and pathogenesis of epilepsy. *NY J. Med.*, 101:567–573, 623–628.

Comings, D. E., & Comings, B. G. (1982), A case of familial exhibitionism in Tourette's syndrome successfully treated with haloperidol. *Amer. J. Psychiatry*, 139:913–915.

Culebras, A., & Moore, J. T. (1989), Magnetic resonance findings in REM sleep behavior disorder. *Neurology*, 39:1519–1523.

Daniels, L. E. (1934), Narcolepsy. *Medicine*, 13:1–122.

Dement, W., & Kleitman, N. (1957), Cyclic variations in EEG during sleep and their relation to eye movements, body motility and dreaming. *Electroenceph. Clin. Neurophysiol.*, 9:673–690.

—— Rechtschaffen, A., & Gulevich, G. (1966), The nature of the narcoleptic sleep attack. *Neurology*, 16:18–33.

Drake, Jr., M. E. (1988), Cotard's syndrome and temporal lobe epilepsy. *Psychiat. J. Univ. Ottawa*, 13:36–39.

Efron, R. (1957), The conditioned inhibition of uncinate fits. *Brain*, 80:251–262.

Epstein, A. W. (1961), Relationship of fetishism and transvestism to brain and particularly to temporal lobe dysfunction. *J. Nerv. Ment. Dis.*, 133:247–253.

—— (1964), Recurrent dreams: Their relationship to temporal lobe seizures. *Arch. Gen. Psychiatry*, 10:25–30.

—— (1966), Contribution of epileptic phenomena to the study of memory mechanisms. *Bull. Tulane Med Fac.*, 25:305–309.

—— (1967), Body image alterations during seizures and dreams of epileptics. *Arch. Neurol.*, 16:613–619.

—— (1969), Fetishism: A comprehensive view. In: *Science and Psychoanalysis*, Vol. 15, ed. J. H. Masserman. New York: Grune & Stratton, pp. 81–87.

—— (1973a), The relationship of altered brain states to sexual psychopathology. In: *Contemporary Sexual Behavior: Critical Issues in the 1970s*, ed. J. Zubin & J. Money. Baltimore: Johns Hopkins University Press, pp. 297–310.

—— (1973b), The typical dream: Case studies. *J. Nerv. Ment. Dis.*, 156:47–56.

—— (1975), The fetish object: Phylogenetic considerations. *Arch. Sexual Behav.*, 4:303–308.

—— (1977), Dream formation during an epileptic seizure: Implications for the study of the "unconscious." *J. Amer. Acad. Psychoanal.*, 5:43–49.

—— (1979), Effect of certain cerebral hemispheric diseases on dreaming. *Biol. Psychiatry*, 14:77–93.

—— (1982), Mental phenomena across generations: The holocaust. *J. Amer. Acad. Psychoanal.*, 10:565–570.

—— (1985), The waking event-dream interval. *Amer. J. Psychiatry*, 142:123–124.

—— (1985–1986), Complex behavioral chains of temporo-limbic epilepsy and their relationship to emotional phylogenesis: Ictal laughter. *Internat. J. Neurol.*, 19–20:127–132.

—— (1987a), Observations on maternal protective behavior derived from unconscious phenomena. *J. Amer. Acad. Psychoanal.*, 15:407–414.

—— (1987b), The phylogenetics of fetishism. In: *Variant Sexuality: Research and Theory*, ed. G. D. Wilson. London & Sydney: Croom Helm, pp. 142–149.

—— (1987–1988), Can memories be encoded across generations? *Internat. J. Neurol.*, 21–22:105–108.

—— (1988), Obligatory associations: A function of dreaming. *Amer. J. Psychiatry*, 145:365–366.

—— (1990), What the reflex epilepsies reveal about the physiology of ideation. *J. Neuropsychiat. Clin. Neurosci.*, 2:69–71.

—— (1992), Categorization: A fundamental of unconscious mental activity. *J. Amer. Acad. Psychoanal.*, 20:91–98.

—— (1992), Common human phobias. *J. Louisiana State Med. Soc.*, 144:329–330.

—— (1994), Searching for the neural correlates of associative structures. *Perspect. in Biol. & Med.*, 37:339–346.

—— Collie, W. R. (1976), Is there a genetic factor in certain dream types? *Biol. Psychiatry*, 11:359–362.

—— Ervin, F. (1956), Psychodynamic significance of seizure content in psychomotor epilepsy. *Psychosom. Med.*, 18:43–55.

—— Freeman, N. R. (1981), The uncinate focus and dreaming. *Epilepsia*, 22:603–605.

—— Hill, W. (1966), Ictal phenomena during REM sleep of a temporal lobe epileptic. *Arch. Neurol.*, 15:367–375.

—— Simmons, N. N. (1983), Aphasia with reported loss of dreaming. *Amer. J. Psychiatry*, 140:108–109.

Epstein, H. (1979), *Children of the Holocaust*. New York: G. P. Putnam's.

Faingold, C. L. (1992), Neuronal networks, epilepsy and the action of antiepileptic drugs. In: *Drugs for Control of Epilepsy: Actions on Neuronal Networks Involved in Seizure Disorders*, ed. C. L. Faingold & G. H. Fromm. Boca Raton, FL: CRC Press, pp. 1–21.

Ferguson, S. M., Rayport, M., Gardner, R., Kass, W., Weiner, H., & Reiser, M. F. (1969), Similarities in mental content of psychotic states, spontaneous seizures, dreams, and responses to electrical brain stimulation in patients with temporal lobe epilepsy. *Psychosom. Med.*, 31:479–498.

Foulkes, D. (1978), *A Grammar of Dreams.* New York: Basic Books.

Frazer, J. G. (1922), *The New Golden Bough*, abridged ed., ed. T. H. Gaster. New York: New American Library, 1964.

Freud, S. (1891), *On Aphasia.* New York: International Universities Press, 1953.

—— (1900), The Interpretation of Dreams. *Standard Edition*, 4 & 5. London: Hogarth Press, 1953.

—— (1909a), Analysis of a phobia in a five-year-old boy. *Standard Edition*, 10:3–147. London: Hogarth Press, 1955.

—— (1909b), Notes upon a case of obsessional neurosis. *Standard Edition*, 10:153–318. London: Hogarth Press, 1955.

—— (1913), Totem and Taboo. *Standard Edition*, 13:1–161. London: Hogarth Press, 1955.

—— (1927), Fetishism. *Collected Papers*, 5. London: Hogarth Press, pp. 198–204, 1950.

Gaffney, G. R., Lurie, S. F., & Berlin, F. S. (1984), Is there familial transmission of pedophilia? *J. Nerv. Ment. Dis.*, 172:546–548.

Gardner, Jr., R., Grossman, W. I., Roffwarg, H. P., & Weiner, H. (1975), The relationship of small limb movements during REM sleep to dreamed limb action. *Psychosom. Med.*, 37:147–158.

Goldie, L., & Green, J. M. (1959), A study of the psychological factors in a case of sensory reflex epilepsy. *Brain*, 82:505–524.

Gorman, G. F. (1964), Fetishism occurring in identical twins. *Brit. J. Psychiatry*, 110:255–256.

Greenberg, R., & Dewan, E. M. (1969), Aphasia and rapid eye movement sleep. *Nature*, 223:183–184.

Grof, S. (1985), *Beyond the Brain.* Albany: State University of New York Press.

Hart, Jr., J., Berndt, R. S., & Caramazza, A. (1985), Category-specific naming deficit following cerebral infarction. *Nature*, 316:439–440.

Head, H. (1926), *Aphasia and Kindred Disorders of Speech.* New York: Hafner, 1963.

Heath, R. G. (1954), *Studies in Schizophrenia.* Cambridge, MA: Harvard University Press.

Hendricks, J. C., Morrison, A. R., & Mann, G. L. (1982), Different behaviors during paradoxical sleep without atonia depend on pontine lesion site. *Brain Res.*, 239:81–105.

Hill, D., & Mitchell, W. (1953), Epileptic anamnesis. *Folia Psychiat.*, 56:718–725.

Hobson, J. A., & McCarley, R. W. (1977), The brain as a dream state generator: An activation-synthesis hypothesis of the dream process. *Amer. J. Psychiatry*, 134:1335–1348.

Hodgson, A. G. O. (1926), Dreams in Central Africa. *Man*, 26:66–68.

Hoffman, R. E., Oates, E., Hafner, R. J., Hustig, H. H., & McGlashan, T. H. (1994), Semantic organization of hallucinated "voices" in schizophrenia. *Amer. J. Psychiatry*, 151:1229–1230.

Humphrey, M. E., & Zangwill, O. L. (1951), Cessation of dreaming after brain injury. *J. Neurol. Neurosurg. Psychiatry*, 14:322–325.

Hunter, R., Logue, V., & McMenemy, W. H. (1963), Temporal lobe epilepsy supervening on longstanding transvestism and fetishism. *Epilepsia*, 4:60–65.

Ionasescu, V. (1960), Paroxysmal disorders of the body image in temporal lobe epilepsy. *Acta Psychiat. Neurol. Scand.*, 35:171–181.

Jackson, J. H. (1882), On some implications of dissolution of the nervous system. *Medical Press and Circular*, 2:44. In: *Selected Writings of John Hughlings Jackson*, ed. J. Taylor. New York: Basic Books, 1958.

—— (1888), On a particular variety of epilepsy ("intellectual aura"), one case with symptoms of organic brain disease. *Brain*, 11:179–207. In: *Selected Writings of John Hughlings Jackson*, ed. J. Taylor. New York: Basic Books, 1958.

—— (1890), Case of tumor of the right temporo-sphenoidal lobe, bearing on the localization of the sense of smell and on the interpretation of a particular variety of epilepsy. *Brain*, 12:346–357. In: *Selected Writings of John Hughlings Jackson*, ed. J. Taylor. New York: Basic Books, 1958.

—— (1958), *Selected Writings of John Hughlings Jackson*, ed. J. Taylor. New York: Basic Books.

Jung, C. G. (1953), Two essays on analytical psychology. In: *Collected Works of C. G. Jung*, Vol. 7, ed. H. Read, M. Fordham, & G. Adler. New York: Pantheon.

Kanemoto, K., & Janz, D. (1989), The temporal sequence of aura-sensations in patients with complex focal seizures with particular attention to ictal aphasia. *J. Neurol. Neurosurg. Psychiatry*, 52:52–56.

Kardiner, A. (1932), The bio-analysis of the epileptic reaction. *Psychoanal Quart.*, 1:375–483.

Kestenberg, J. S. (1972), Psychoanalytic contributions to the problem of children of survivors from Nazi persecution. *Isr. Ann. Psychiatry*, 10:311–325.

Krueger, D. W. (1978), Symptom passing in a transvestite father and three sons. *Amer. J. Psychiatry*, 135:739–742.

Kubie, L. S. (1953), Some implications for psychoanalysis of modern concepts of the organization of the brain. *Psychoanal. Quart.*, 22:21–52.

Laycock, T. (1876), Reflex, automatic, and unconscious cerebration: A history and a criticism. *J. Ment. Science*, 21:477–498.

Lesse, H., Heath, R. G., Mickle, W. A., Monroe, R. R., & Miller, W. H. (1955), Rhinencephalic activity during thought. *J. Nerv. Ment. Dis.*, 122:433–440.

Lewis, A. (1935), Problems of obsessional illness. *Proc. Royal Soc. Med.*, 29:325–336.

Lief, H. I. (1955), Sensory association in the selection of phobic objects. *Psychiatry*, 18:331–338.

Little, R. B. (1967), Spider phobias. *Psychoanal. Quart.*, 36:51–60.

Luciano, D., Devinsky, O., & Perrine, K. (1993), Crying seizures. *Neurology*, 43:2113–2117.

Mandler, J. M., & Mandler, G. (1964), *Thinking: From Association to Gestalt*. New York: John Wiley.

Marks, I. M., Crowe, M., Drewe, E., Young, J., & Dewhurst, W. G. (1969), Obsessive compulsive neurosis in identical twins. *Brit. J. Psychiatry*, 115:991–998.

McKenna, P., & Warrington, E. K. (1978), Category-specific naming preservation: A single case study. *J. Neurol. Neurosurg. Psychiatry*, 41:571–574.

Mill, J. (1878), *Analysis of the Phenomena of the Human Mind*, Vol. 1, 2nd ed. London: Longmans, Green, Reader, & Dyer.

Mitchell, W., Falconer, M. A., & Hill, D. (1954), Epilepsy with fetishism relieved by temporal lobectomy. *Lancet*, 2:626–630.

Nadelson, T. (1992), Attachment to killing. *J. Amer. Acad. Psychoanal.*, 20:130–141.

Nausieda, P. A., Weiner, W. J., Kaplan, L. R., Weber, S., & Klawans, H. L. (1982), Sleep disruption in the course of chronic levodopa therapy: An early feature of the levodopa psychosis. *Clin. Neuropharm.*, 5:183–194.

Niederland, W. G. (1968), Clinical observations on the "survivor syndrome." *Internat. J. Psycho-Anal.*, 49:313–315.

Offen, M. L., Davidoff, R. A., Troost, B. T., & Richey, E. T. (1976), Dacrystic epilepsy. *J. Neurol. Neurosurg. Psychiatry*, 39:829–834.

Palombo, S. R. (1978), *Dreaming and Memory: A New Information-Processing Model*. New York: Basic Books.

—— (1984), Recovery of early memories associated with reported dream imagery. *Amer. J. Psychiatry*, 141:1508–1511.

Pavlov, I. P. (1957), *Experimental Psychology and Other Essays*. New York: Philosophical Library.

Payne, S. M. (1939), Some observations on the ego development of the fetishist. *Internat. J. Psycho-Anal.*, 20:161–170.

Penfield, W., & Jasper, H. (1954), *Epilepsy and the Functional Anatomy of the Human Brain*. Boston: Little, Brown.

—— Rasmussen, T. (1950), *The Cerebral Cortex of Man*. New York: Macmillan.

Pitman, R. K. (1988), Post-traumatic stress disorder, conditioning, and network theory. *Psychiatric Ann.*, 18:182–189.

Rado, S. (1949), Mind, unconscious mind and brain. *Psychosom. Med.*, 11:165–168.

—— (1956), Adaptational psychodynamics: A basic science. In: *Psychoanalysis of Behavior: Collected Papers*, Vol. 1. New York: Grune & Stratton, pp. 332–346.

Reami, D. O., Silva, D. F., Albuquerque, M., & Campos, C. J. R. (1991), Dreams and epilepsy. *Epilepsia*, 32:51–53.

Rodin, E. A., Mulder, D. W., Faucett, R. L., & Bickford, R. G. (1955), Psychologic factors in convulsive disorders of focal orgin. *AMA Arch. Neurol. Psychiatry*, 74:365–374.

Roy, A. (1983), Family history of suicide. *Arch. Gen. Psychiatry*, 40:971–974.

Sanders, D. G. (1973), Familial occurrence of Gilles de la Tourette syndrome: Report of the syndrome occurring in a father and son. *Arch. Gen. Psychiatry*, 28:326–328.

Sastre, J.-P., & Jouvet, M. (1979), Le comportement onirique du chat. *Physiol. Behav.*, 22:979–989.

Schenck, C. H., Bundlie, S. R., & Mahowald, M. W. (1985), Human REM sleep chronic behavior disorders: A new category of parasomnia. *Sleep Res.*, 14:208.

—— Hurwitz, T. D., & Mahowald, M. W. (1988), REM sleep behavior disorder. *Amer. J. Psychiatry*, 145:652.

Schneider, D. M., & Sharp, L. (1971), *The Dream Life of a Primitive People: The Dreams of the Yir Yoront of Australia.* Ann Arbor, MI: University Microfilms.

Shapiro, E. R. (1980), Children's sensitivity to projective identification. *Amer. J. Psychiatry*, 137:506.

Shobe, F. O., & Gildea, M. C.-L. (1968), Long-term follow-up of selected lobotomized private patients. *J. Amer. Med. Assn.*, 206:327–332.

Solomon, K. (1983), Thiothixene and bizarre nightmares: An association? *J. Clin. Psychiatry*, 44:77–78.

Solursh, L. (1988), Combat addiction: Post-traumatic stress disorder re-explored. *Psychiatric J. Univ. Ottawa*, 13:17–20.

Solyom, L., Beck, P., Solyom, C., & Hugel, R. (1974), Some etiological factors in phobic neurosis. *Can. Psychiatric Assn. J.*, 19:69–78.

Sperling, M. (1952), Animal phobias in a two-year-old child. *The Psychoanalytic Study of the Child*, 7:115–125. New York: International Universities Press.

—— (1964), A case of ophidiophilia. *Internat. J. Psycho-Anal.*, 45:227–233.

Stevens, J. R. (1957), The "march" of temporal lobe epilepsy. *AMA Arch. Neurol. Psychiatry*, 77:227–236.

Stewart, J. T., & Bartucci, R. J. (1986), Posttraumatic stress disorder and partial complex seizures. *Amer. J. Psychiatry*, 143:113–114.

Stoller, R. J. (1980), Obituaries: Ralph R. Greenson. *Internat. J. Psycho-Anal.*, 61:559–560.

Strunz, F. (1993), Preconscious mental activity and scientific problem-solving: A critique of the Kekulé dream controversy. *Dreaming*, 3:281–294.

Tuke, D. H. (1894), Imperative ideas. *Brain*, 17:179–197.

Van Valkenburgh, B., & Hertel, F. (1993), Tough times at La Brea: Tooth breakage in large carnivores of the late pleistocene. *Science*, 261:456–459.

Ward, C. H., Beck, A. T., & Rascoe, E. (1961), Typical dreams. *Arch Gen. Psychiatry*, 5:116–125.

Wardi, D. (1992), *Memorial Candles: Children of the Holocaust*. London: Routledge.

Warrington, E. K., & McCarthy, R. (1983), Category specific access dysphasia. *Brain*, 106:859–878.

—— Shallice, T. (1984), Category specific semantic impairments. *Brain*, 107:829–854.

Williams, D. (1956), The structure of emotions reflected in epileptic experiences. *Brain*, 79:29–67.

Winnik, H. Z. (1968), Contribution to symposium on psychic traumatization through social catastrophe. *Internat. J. Psycho-Anal.*, 49:298–301.

Wood, J. M., & Bootzin, R. R. (1990), The prevalence of nightmares and their independence from anxiety. *J. Abnorm. Psychology*, 99:64–68.

Woodruff, R., & Pitts, Jr., F. N. (1964), Monozygotic twins with obsessional illness. *Amer. J. Psychiatry*, 120:1075–1080.

Zaw, K. M. (1981), A suicidal family. *Brit. J. Psychiatry*, 139:68–69.

Author Index

Subject Index

171